DARK PSYCHOLOGY & MANIPULATION

Lead Your Psychological Warfare by Discovering Advanced Secrets to Manipulate Your Clients & Relationships Using Emotional Intelligence, NLP and the Art of Persuasion

Blake Reyes

is the solitary and utter responsibility of the recipient reader. Under no circumstances will any legal responsibility or blame be held against the publisher for any reparation, damages, or monetary loss due to the information herein, either directly or indirectly.

Respective authors own all copyrights not held by the publisher.

The information herein is offered for informational purposes solely and is universal as so. The presentation of the information is without contract or any type of guarantee assurance.

The trademarks that are used are without any consent, and the publication of the trademark is without permission or backing by the trademark owner. All trademarks and brands within this book are for clarifying purposes only and are the owned by the owners themselves, not affiliated with this document.

TABLE OF CONTENTS

INTRODUCTION 9
CHAPTER 1 - WHAT'S DARK PSYCHOLOGY? 11
CHAPTER 2 - THE 4 DARK PSYCHOLOGY TRAITS..... 13
   Narcissist.. 13
   Machiavellian.. 14
   Psychopaths and Sociopaths 16
   Sadism.. 17
CHAPTER 3 - DO WE ALL HAVE A DARK SIDE?........ 21
CHAPTER 4 - THE DARK SIDE OF JOKER 29
CHAPTER 5 - MASKS PEOPLE WEAR 36
CHAPTER 6 - PSYCHOLOGICAL WARFARE.............. 73
   How to Enter Your Clients' Mind 84
   5 Techniques to Read People 87
CHAPTER 7 - BEHAVIORAL AND CHARACTER
TRAITS OF MANIPULATORS 93
   Shake Your Confidence 93
   Projecting the Blame... 96
   Play the Victim 101
CHAPTER 8 - PSYCHOLOGICAL MANIPULATION
TECHNIQUES... 108
   Learn How to Avoid Their Manipulation
   Techniques.. 110
CHAPTER 9 - THE ROLE OF DEFENCE 115
   Why is being assertive so important 119
   What is an assertive response? 121
CHAPTER 10 - THE POWER OF EMOTIONAL
INTELLIGENCE 127
   What Is Emotional Intelligence?....................... 127
   Main Elements of Emotional Intelligence......... 130

Habits of People with High Emotional
Intelligence 134
Emotional Intelligence can be developed 139
Busting the Myths About Emotional
Intelligence 141
CHAPTER 11 - WHY DO YOU NEED EMOTIONAL
INTELLIGENCE IN YOUR BUSINESS? 146
Why Is Emotional Intelligence Important in
The Workplace?...................................148
Emotionally Intelligent People Handle
Pressure Better....................................151
Emotionally Intelligent People Are Better
Decision-Makers 155
Five Ways Emotional Intelligence Helps You
Make Decisions....................................157
People with High EQ Handle Conflicts Better ...158
CHAPTER 12 - THE ART OF PERSUASION..............162
The History of Persuasion...................................168
Persuasion 101 171
Discover When You Are the Target 173
Behavioral Traits of Manipulation 178
CHAPTER 13 - HOW TO RECOGNIZE DOUBLE-
FACED PEOPLE.......................................183
How to deal with Double-faced people?...........191
CHAPTER 14 - DARK PERSUASION METHODS 193
CHAPTER 15 - NEURO-LINGUISTIC
PROGRAMMING 198
What is Neuro-linguistic Programming? 198
Verbal vs. Non-Verbal Communication 204
NLP To Influence....................................207
NLP Techniques You Must Master 211

CHAPTER 16 - BODY LANGUAGE 101 217
  Make Body Language Your Superpower........... 226
CHAPTER 17 - HYPNOSIS 101.............................. 230
CHAPTER 18 - HYPNOTHERAPY 238
  How effective is hypnotherapy?...................... 241
  Why do few people get involved in
  hypnotherapy?... 241
  Where to find psychologists trained in
  hypnosis 243
CHAPTER 19 - BRAINWASHING 245
  What Is Brainwashing? 246
  Brainwashing in the 21st Century.................... 247
CHAPTER 20 - SOCIAL INFLUENCE 253
  Intended Social Influence or Persuasion 254
  Typologies in The Study of Influence............... 254
  Influence techniques....................................... 255
CHAPTER 21 - THE SECRETS OF SUBLIMINAL
PSYCHOLOGY 258
  Subliminal Psychology in An Intimate
  Relationship 262
CHAPTER 22 - HOW TO USE DARK PSYCHOLOGY
IN SEDUCTION 264
CHAPTER 23 - CONCLUSION 267

INTRODUCTION

Congratulations on reading Manipulation and thank you for doing so.

There are plenty of books on this subject on the market, thanks again for choosing this one! Every effort was made to ensure it is full of as much useful information as possible, and please enjoy it!

Any wise driver will let one of his passengers take the steering wheel in his place to drive and go wherever he wants. That is what happens if we are threatened or tampered with. Someone harshly or insidiously wants one to perceive, behave, work, or love as he or she wishes. The manipulator invades and thus destroys an essential part of our lives by using techniques that paralyze us, confuse us, or prevent us from reacting. One day, you're happy and confident, and on another day, irritable, nervous, or apathetic, you might think life is so unfair. You may start crying, feel guilty or crumble, and feel depressed and lonely. But that doesn't affect anything that makes you nervous or frustrated.

For instance, when one is overworked or, on the contrary, when one is fearful of being robbed of work, it is common to encounter moments of discouragement. In the face of defeat, confrontation, disease, or an otherwise bleak condition, it is equally acceptable to lose faith or to have doubts. Sometimes, however, these symptoms often stem directly from some form of manipulation.

Some manipulations are so twisted or concealed that the victim is often unable to identify the cause. She falsely blames herself and discusses how she may be accountable for what has happened to her. Other manipulations, on the other hand, are simple, but we also realize we won't be able to fight the manipulator and eventually give in to him.

This book is intended for all those who are tired of walking on their feet, sufficient to be too kind or too nice, sufficient to be sad enough to be able to live their lives. The book is, in essence, about those sick of being abused.

CHAPTER 1

WHAT'S DARK PSYCHOLOGY?

Dark psychology can be understood as the study of the human condition based on the psychological nature of the different types of people who take advantage of others. The fact is that every human being has the potential to victimize other people or other living creatures. However, due to social norms, human consciousness, and other factors, most humans tend to contain their dark impulses and avoid acting for every impulse they have. However, there is a small percentage of the population who cannot control their darkest instincts and harm others in apparent unimaginable ways.

What kinds of traits do malicious and exploitative people have? What are the psychological impulses that lead people to act contrary to social norms and harmful to others?

With Dark Manipulation and Psychology, you will learn to know if the people in your life have bad intentions towards you. Or if new love interests that seem charming at first are likely to turn into selfish and manipulative people once you've let them into your life.

The dark triad describes the interaction of the following personality traits:

- Narcissism
- Machiavellianism
- Psychopathy
- Sadism

All of these personality traits can be found in different forms of people. The commonality is that they are all selfish and elevate their good to that of others. The three types differ mainly in their motivation. The narcissist is about admiration, the Machiavellist wants to achieve his goals, and the psychopath is about the action itself.

A certainly increased amount of this is a success factor in our society (managers). However, over-expression is devastating and has destructive effects on the environment, which even companies cannot wish for. In the meantime, the term "dark triad" is also used in the assessment and selection of executives in companies in the "toolbox."

The concept of the dark triad was coined by the Canadian psychologists DL Paulhus and KM Williams in 2002.

CHAPTER 2

THE 4 DARK PSYCHOLOGY TRAITS

People can be classified according to their personality, and the traits that compose it. Different types are differentiated by their way of acting, self-confidence, and the way they deal with others.

Just as there are different ways of being, there are also personality disorders that are dangerous and harmful. In this section, we look at the four types of personalities that science calls dark.

Narcissist

Narcissist or being narcissistic is related to narcissism. According to Greek myth, Narcissus was a beautiful young man full of pride, vanity, and callousness who despised all the maidens and others who fell in love with him.

Nemesis, the goddess of revenge, punished Narcissus. When he saw himself reflected in the water of a fountain, he fell in love with his image. He ended up consuming himself in his unsatisfied desire since he was unable to separate himself from his image, which faded every time he tried to reach out to kiss her. Narcissus, saddened by pain, commits suicide with his sword and, after dying, falls into the water and transforms into the flower that bears his name, the narcissus, a beautiful smelly but sterile flower of fruit.

Therefore, a narcissist is a person who feels excessive admiration for himself, for his physical appearance and his gifts or qualities. A narcissist par excellence is an egocentric person, and proud to the point of not being able to live a happy life. This is because he shows a sharp egoism and a disregard for the needs and feelings of others which can become perverse.

We all know quite a number of narcissists, people who stand out for having high self-esteem and little or no concern for the feelings of others since they will always take first place.

Narcissists are always thirsty for attention and show that they are superior to the rest. Perhaps at first glance, you do not realize that you are before one, but by knowing him better, you will be able to distinguish the features of this type of dark and toxic personality.

Machiavellian

Nicolas Machiavelli (1469 - 1527), political

philosopher and author of The Prince, wrote, "A wise ruler must never keep the faith when doing so would be against his interests," and "a prince is never short of good reasons to break his or her promise".

In Machiavelli's opinion, honesty, and all the other virtues are dispensable if deception, betrayal, and force are more convenient. In short, people in positions of power must choose to be Machiavellian, even if that is not their usual style of leadership.

In Psychology, Machiavellianism refers to a personality type that does not choose to be but simply is a master of manipulation. The Machiavellian people do not have to read The Prince to acquire the knack for deception.

They are biased as far as temperament is concerned to be calculating, confusing, and deceitful. In essence, amoral, that other people use as steppingstones to reach their goals. From a Machiavellian perspective, if we allow ourselves to be used, we probably deserve it. PT Barnum expresses this way of thinking when he said, "There's a sucker born every minute."

The "end justifies the means"; that phrase from Nicolas Machiavelli perfectly illustrates the type of personality that bears his name. The main characteristic of Machiavellians is that they are excellent manipulators and very intelligent.

A Machiavellian knows no limits when it comes to getting what he wants and easily convinces others to act even illegally to fulfill what he or she wants, just as if they were disposable pawns in a game of chess.

A Machiavellian person is more difficult to detect than narcissists, and they are often more dangerous.

Psychopaths and Sociopaths

The most dangerous of all dark personalities, psychopathy is an important part of serial killers who are characterized by their cruelty and not only lack of empathy with the suffering of the other, but also enjoying the evil of others.

Although psychopaths and sociopaths fall under the same dark personality classification, psychopaths will sooner or later act as it is very difficult for them to control their impulses. The sociopath is more intelligent, and although he enjoys the suffering of others and causing pain, he goes more for the psychological rather than the physical side.

A sociopath can live perfectly well without committing crimes, making them more difficult to detect. In addition to dark personalities, both are considered a harmful disorder which makes them dangerous to society since there is no way to reform them, and they are born that way.

Sadism

Sadism is a word derived from Donatien Alphonse François de Sade, better known as Marquis de Sade. He is a writer and philosopher who was born in 1740 and died in 1814 and who remained in history for narrating various paraphilia and vices.

The notion of sadism, in this way, is used to name the perversion that consists of obtaining pleasure from exercising cruelty on another living being. The sadist, therefore, enjoys causing pain to others.

The usual thing is to associate sadism with the sexual: the sadist gets excited and gets pleasure from humiliating the other or generating some type of damage. Arousal is produced by humiliation and harm, and not by the sexual practice itself.

Tying the sexual victim with handcuffs, spanking, or locking them are some of the behaviors of sadism. The sadist can also resort to rape his victim.

In addition to all the above, we cannot ignore other important aspects related to sadism, such as these:

-It becomes negative paraphilia as long as it produces damage to third parties.

-According to the studies carried out in this regard, it has been shown that, after studying the brain of sadists, they have a very high sensitivity regarding what other people's pain is. Specifically, this conclusion has been reached after checking how the amygdala, which processes reactions to what emotions are, was activated in the brains of these individuals when they saw images of suffering and violence.

-Many people practice sadism with their partners because both parties agree and accept it. However, they must take certain precautions and impose certain limits since some actions can directly be very dangerous and cause serious damage to one of them, including death. We are referring to actions such as beating, raping, electric shock, torture, trying to strangle her...

-It is considered that there are a series of disorders that are associated with a certain frequency to what sadism is. We are referring to depressive disorder, antisocial disorder, narcissistic personality disorder... In some cases, we can establish that, in addition to all the above, it can also be associated with the consumption of psychoactive substances.

Beyond sexuality, sadism is understood as an act of cruelty that a person performs for his delight. A man who mistreats a dog for fun will be incurring sadism: his action generates joy from the suffering of the animal.

He who kidnaps a child, locks him in a room without light or ventilation, denies him food, and only enters the room to hit his victim, will also be developing behavior of great sadism since he does not seek anything other than to take pleasure in the abuse he exercises.

We could consider sadism to be one of the characteristics of the dark personalities that we have already named, but a sadist takes his actions much further than in other cases.

The sadist enjoys causing the greatest amount of suffering in the other and at a higher level of cruelty. Their difference from psychopaths is that sadists are not impulsive.

People with a sadistic personality seek to belong to groups or have jobs where they have power over the application of control and violence over others.

A sadist is dangerous, but sadly he knows how to hide his actions as well.

It is not necessary to gather all the traits to belong to one of these groups of dark personalities since, like everything in human psychology, it is presented in different degrees and not all reach the most harmful and dangerous level.

CHAPTER 3

DO WE ALL HAVE A DARK SIDE?

If, to save one of your loved ones, you had to accept that the heart of a serial killer be grafted in him, would you accept? Before you answer, think about it... Can we say that a serial killer has "a heart"?

In all cases, from a medical and scientific point of view, this is impossible since organ donations are made anonymously, and neither the name of the donor nor the name of the recipient is given to families.

The question we should ask ourselves is rather: what makes a person coldly attack someone for the simple "pleasure" of killing?

Are we the product of evil?

According to Catharism (a religious movement which appeared in the 12th century, spread mainly in the South of France and inspired by ancient Eastern pagan beliefs based on the doctrine of Good and Evil), Man is the product of Evil.

Believers relied so much on this doctrine that they even condemned procreation because they believed that having children would only cause more Evil.

One might think that it is sordid to say that Man is the product of Evil. However, unfortunately, it is enough to look out the window, read the newspapers, or listen to the radio to see that Man is well capable of evil acts.

This, therefore, demonstrates that humanity has a predisposition to Evil and that if we allow ourselves to be guided by our instincts, the consequences would be catastrophic.

The society helps calm our aggressive instincts

Whether we like it or not, society is an entity made up of all of us. This society functions as a kind of mechanism which needs to follow rules to function.

For example, we depend on the behavior of our neighbor and his way of life. If he doesn't put the music on loud at night, then there will be no conflicts.

My colleague depends on my good humor at work. So, I don't upset his testosterone levels, and nothing trivial will affect the rest of his day. On the contrary, if the day goes wrong, he insults me, I tell others, the news spreads, and a negative atmosphere prevails at work.

And if serotonin calms the worst urges, testosterone can cause many men to commit the worst acts ever imagined, and that from a very small spark. Don't be that spark!

Fight our inner monster

It is certain that we will never be able to forget that blood flows in our veins. And that, very often, when all is well, there is always someone to play with our nerves (an insult a little too much, an attack on our physical integrity, etc.), but that doesn't mean it will always be like that.

Indeed, the balance and the good harmony of society will sometimes be altered by our fault (whether we realize it or not).

According to a recent study by the University of Beihang (China), anger is the emotion that spreads the most when it is exposed to social networks, unlike cheerful and kind SMSs.

All the more reason to continue following the example of our neighbor, but also to remember that our worst enemy guides our instinct: ourselves.

Fighting against your "inner self" is a daily task. At times, you will feel overwhelmed by this "inner self" when he shows the fangs, and brings out his anger, sarcasm, and venom.

This struggle will affect not only your relationship with others but also your desires to be happy and to live. This monster in us can be terrible. Some people don't even know it, but if it does surface one day, it will terrorize more than one.

Thus, people who know their " inner monster " must be more careful, more tolerant, calmer, and sometimes lenient enough not to wake him up and threaten the lives of innocent people in their path.

If only no one had an inner monster! However, the fact of living with him makes us aware of who we are, of our limits and our faults, and curiously of all the positive things to share.

Because even if, according to Ernest Hemingway, " It is always in innocence that real evil takes its source," Martin Luther King Jr. reminds us that, " To resolve human conflicts, we must exclude violence, and the spirit of revenge. The solution is love."

Explore the dark side to regain self-discipline

Were you hateful? Do you do things you're afraid to be thinking about? Is there a part of you that you want to do away with? Would you want to say things you hate? We do have a dark side we are afraid to face.

The cynical side is not stolen from good thoughts, sacrifices, stuff we have to do. He is marginalized, and since he is struggling for a way out, he grows in you.

Exploring the dark side will make it easier for you to take control of yourself, understand yourself, and learn about yourself.

What does your dark side feed on?

The dark side of your mind feeds on misery and self-destruction, all that you deny of yourself, and those desires that you cannot manage to materialize.

Your unmet needs produce negative emotions that fuel them. If you fail to get these needs out, these negative emotions will grow in you, and this will bring out the worst in you.

Therefore, you will think it is the real version of yourself or even that it is the only one.

Not feeding this dark part of your mind is the only way to control it.

However, there are many things you know you should not do because they are bad for you, but you do them anyway.

You know you shouldn't smoke, that you shouldn't abuse fats, that you shouldn't quarrel with your spouse or children, that you shouldn't fuel unnecessary arguments, but you do it anyway.

Your dark side is not made of good intentions, either. Either you take action and stop feeding it, or it will take control of you.

What does your dark side need?

To stop feeding your dark side, you must know what it likes the most. It feeds on negative psychological attachments. These feelings that make you cling forcefully to a previous state that creates anxiety in you.

These negative attachments keep you from feeling secure, balanced, and strong. They are expressed through rejection, humiliation, betrayal, feelings of worthlessness, and failure.

All of this negativity feeds the darkest part of your psyche, which grows with your negative feelings, thoughts, and behaviors, with the influence that toxic people have had on you and still have on you in your life.

Whenever something negative happens in your life or whenever you remember something that you do not like, your dark side gives pride of place, and it clings to this negativity as if there was no other option.

Consequently, more misery, self-destruction, and negativity arise to fuel it.

How to face the dark side?

The solution to dealing with the dark side of the mind is to train it consciously. There are things that we cannot eliminate but that we can face by familiarizing ourselves with them.

The biggest challenge is to sink into your mind and bring to light everything that is hidden there.

The dark side hides much more than unfulfilled desires, frustrated aspirations, or broken illusions. But each person is the only one who can immerse themselves and explore their dark side.

Whenever negativity arises in your life, and you feel that something dark is trying to gain power over you, it is then that you must discover why, without being ashamed.

You have to accept that there is an obscure side of your mind that is present and that it cannot go up in smoke simply because you will repress it. The repression will make him even stronger, and he will explode with more force as soon as he has the opportunity. Be brave, be honest with yourself, and try to release that negativity from yourself

Meditation and coaching can help. Through art, you can also get the worst out of your mind, by channeling that negativity.

By knowing what your dark side is hiding, you will be able to regain control of your life and learn to manage negativity better so that it does not dominate you.

CHAPTER 4

THE DARK SIDE OF JOKER

The Joker is a film by Todd Philips. He received a golden lion in Venice, with a fabulous Joaquin Phoenix, while generating serious concerns when he left in front of the violence he could inspire. So much so that, in certain American cities, security measures have been decreed to avoid any violence.

This film shows us a clownish character who has never been so close to our lives and who highlights all the fragility of our society. In this film, it is no longer a metaphorical scenario, but a parable which is part of a raw representation of our lives and in a city, Gotham city, which no longer has anything imaginary. Gotham City only becomes the cinematic name for New York.

The joker is a clownish character who ignores all rules, transforming all organizations into a house of cards that can collapse at any moment, and plunging any society into immense insecurity.

We often make an amalgam between the character of the clown and that of the Joker, sometimes at the origin of a coulrophobia (the fear of clowns).

The clown, and in particular, the Augustus, is a theatrical character who says yes to everything to play everything. He plays with contexts to live his life in an emotional emergency and to explore his fragility. For him, a pen can be a spaceship, a gun, a car, etc. It is a philosophy of life that allows him, by his posture, to free himself from the constraints to live on the margins of society. His driving force is curiosity, play, and emotion. The clown is a benevolent cabin, a four-year-old child who wants, in the end, to be loved. We laugh at him out of tenderness and not out of mockery. He does not live against anyone, and he has no claim, he is in the moment. He offers a poetic vision of life by opening other possibilities by recombining what is presented to him: Buffo or Harpo by the Marx Brothers are fine examples. Slava, one of the biggest living clowns, has a house in Seine et Marne, called the Moulin Jaune, that you could visit from time to time. In his garden, you can find cucumber trees that show the sweet poetic madness that the clown offers. The clown is a show character who only has a raison d'être within the show or as the king's jester.

The Joker is the dark side of the force. It is the antithesis of our society as black is the antithesis of white, the emptiness of the full. It can only exist because a certain society exists. Besides, in the movie Dark Knight, he says that he only exists because Batman exists. The more Batman tries to find solutions to save the world, the more the Joker exists in his shadow.

Our society connects men using rules, dogmas, laws, or morals. All these elements are stories that are told as so well written by Yuval Noah Harari in his book "Sapiens." For example, banknotes have only the value that we give them through the monetary history that we tell. In the past, this story was supported by shells, quantities of wheat, etc. For this story to work, it requires that all men believe the same story. Yuval Noah Harari shows that the stories that men tell themselves since the dawn of time are only a theater and that at any time, another theater can replace it. Likewise, in the games of mistreatment between an executioner and a slave, the two characters must exist. It is enough that one no longer wants to take on the role of the slave so that very often, the executioner no longer exists. The film "Yes but" by Yves Lavandier highlights all of these plays in particular within the families who organize our suffering.

The Joker gives himself the freedom not to believe in these stories, which makes the societal cement, and he allows himself to emancipate it all the more since the law of men has treated him badly, to express his impulses and his desires brutally. In Todd Philips' Joker story, Arthur Fleck, before becoming the Joker, was beaten, humiliated and kicked out for free by men, without doing anything to deserve it. The Joker is born from men's violence and its absurdity.

Depending on the context, in our city, the Joker is:

- A psychopath who ignores the rules in a world so complicated and empty of meaning. This world is a wonderful playground for psychopaths.
- Or a desperate person in an increasingly Kafkaesque world where nothing has any meaning and is not fair.
- Or an idiot who does not see the world from his only perspective, incapable of empathy but capable of violence because he acts from his point of view and that if he thinks it... that means that he is right.

Do you know someone around you who can pin down at any time, and trigger violence? Are not those responsible for the killings in the USA in colleges or cinemas, Jokers?

Our society has become violent because it has lost the sense of what connects men. We are mired in incomprehensible and absurd administrative procedures. At the same time, it has gone astray in consumerism, which studies human beings and in the exploitation of men in savage capitalism for the benefit of belief in growth. Associated with this violence is a spiritual void described by the philosopher Bernard Stiegler. He says that after the Second World War, western society discarded religious spirituality and political spirituality with the retreat from communist ideas. She was unable to replace these binders with the construction of secular spirituality. In our post-modern society, we are freer but more and more alone.

We are more and more equal and, therefore, more and more replaceable. Isn't the crisis of yellow vests the emergence of little jokers who no longer want to participate in this theater? What brought them together was above all to be against, but not the construction of a common project. They never knew how to regroup in a political movement or to stand for election. Moreover, the Yellow Vests of the beginning were excluded, threatened, or even beaten. Within the same roundabout, we could find people who said that we were not helping the poor enough and others who complained that we are helping people too much.

Doesn't the political system by its violence create Jokers? What do people think of people like Trump,

Hollande, Mélenchon, Marine Le Pen...? Aren't they the clowns of our political system? Jacques Chirac is dead, and one has the impression that one has forgotten the bandit that he was at the town hall of Paris. That he was at the origin of the acrobats who beat up the students in 86 and the origin of the death of Malik Oussekine. He spoke about the noise and the smell of certain French, to retain only the sympathetic dimension which sported his puppet of Guignols.

Are Daesh and Osama Bin Laden not the Jokers of our international political games?

In business, how many leaders who go from one business to another are not Jokers at the origin of mistreatment, harassment, and never exposed because they never stay long enough to be spotted?

The Joker is an anti-social psychopath who has no spirituality or morality. He is a disturbing character who shows us the fragility of our society. It is the black hole of our social universe. At any time, it can engulf us.

It is by rediscovering meaning and living together that we will best protect ourselves from it. How to do it without falling into a new religious proposal? Indeed, religion has long participated in social cohesion, and this is what the extremists are trying to replay today by offering us other hells.

The strength of Todd Philips' film is to show us that at any moment, anyone can become an uncontrollable Joker, spreading terror just as Arthur Fleck became the Joker without doing anything.

Todd Philips' film is fascinating, but it sends back the black reflection of what we are, opening the door to all dangers.

CHAPTER 5

MASKS PEOPLE WEAR

The face is not usually a very common philosophical topic. Following the Cartesian route, the rationalist tradition of disembodied thought has prevailed, pure abstraction without anchorage in the situated and concrete corporality. At least until the phenomenological and existential currents—up to Marcel, Sartre and especially, Merleau-Ponty—began to underline precisely that fleshiness, the idea that we are a bodily, mundane, embodied, situated, temporal consciousness. All of them spoke of the "meaning" of the body, not the face in particular. Although as expressive as the body as a whole can be (and it is), it is the face space where that expressiveness and that "meaning" are condensed in the most obvious way. It had to be another philosopher, Emmanuel Levinas, already in the 1960s and fed by these phenomenological sources, as a metaphysical and ethical category.

As valuable and fascinating as the Levinasian contribution is, this chapter takes another point of departure. On the one hand, he understands the face as what makes each human being unique, what makes him or her valuable being visible, what humanism and ethical individualism have praised. On the other hand, he understands the notion of a mask as that which hides that singularity. That which refers it to a type, to a category, to a stereotype, and that which runs the risk of being interchangeable, erasable, expendable. As Jacques Aumont summarizes, "the mask, which tends towards a constructed, social, differentiable, communicating or symbolic typology, makes it difficult to perceive the individual, innate, personal, expressive, projective, empathetic face." Seeing the other in their social masks is a frequent phenomenon, without a doubt, but seeing only the social mask or the type, regardless of the unique, personal face, is the root of any type of racist, classist, sexist, ethnic attitude, etc.: Look at a person and see a Muslim, a gypsy, see a Jew's nose, dark skin, rather than—instead of—a singular face.

This contrast between the individual and unique face and a generic type of face also approximates the opposition of Levinas (1999) between Infinity and Totality. Here, he advocates conceiving the face of the other as Infinite, as a singularity irreducible to concepts. , in such a way that it cannot be subsumed at any time in one's idea of him. That is, by any task of objectification or thematization that makes him dissolve in some form of Totality (always bordering on totalitarianism). Levinas is aware that all the mechanisms of perception that we normally summarize under the notion of vision are conceptualized; they are an immense classification machine. In other words, we generally see faces as masks, veiled, and distorted by our cultural glasses, by the prejudices and stereotypes that serve as cognitive shortcuts to quickly typify others. They are ways of dressing the face, while the true face—which, according to him, "expresses itself," "means" and "visits" us—would be naked.

Now, having established these similarities, we will not follow here the development of the metaphysical ethics elaborated by Levinas.

But we will focus on some aspects of the face/mask contrast, especially in a modern individualistic society, where the recognition of ourselves and the rest is made from our recognition as an individual, beyond our membership in a group, a category or a social role. In this context, the singularity of the face calls the singularity of man as an individual, so that the individual distinction makes a face value, the clearest exponent of our unique and singular being. Of course, the mechanisms of the typification, of the construction of masks, continue to work here.

They would even have been reinforced in the mass society, according to some authors, which leads them to announce a "defeat of the face" that we will analyze and discuss.

For this reflection, we will start from two stories that are rarely related: the revealing etymological history that unites the notions of a person, face and mask, and the history of modern and contemporary portrait that exposes a sample of equally revealing 'faces' and 'masks.' We will end in our contemporary society, trying to compose a balance of the two faces, the dresses, and the nudes, that are offered to us within the empire of the image.

1. Face, mask, person: an etymological history

Face, mask, role, character, person... All those words are intertwined if we stick to their etymological past. Let's start with the classical Greek term for face, prosopon, which means "what is before the eyes of others." The most curious thing for us is that the same word designates, at the same time, the mask (both stage and ritual mask). That is, the Greeks lacked a specific term to differentiate the face of the mask linguistically, nor did they distinguish it iconographically (in the representations of the Greek vessels, there is no demarcation between face and mask).

To understand this indistinction of prosopon, we must bear in mind that the Greek culture is, like all traditional cultures, a culture of face to face, of exteriority, a culture of honor and shame. The individual is apprehended from the outside, by the gaze that the others direct at him. So, the face is a mirror of the soul, yes, but always for others. It does not have in itself the function of hiding; on the contrary, it is the revealer of emotions, of thoughts, of character. Despite Plato's attempts to warn about the confusions between being and appearance, the truth is that in Greek culture, this opposition is not palpable; on the contrary, appearance reveals being, it is Being. And the self-knowledge that is produced necessarily goes through that reciprocity. In essence, they are the side mirrors of others, of the like, where one sees and perceives himself with a certain identity. In fact, in the classical Greek texts, prosopon appears almost always referring to another—your face or his face. The first-person, reflexive cases are exceptional.

So, the prosopon—the mask is the same as the prosopon—face: it is what is presented to the view of others, the visible, in front of the covered parts of the body. Prosopon is always related to looking, with what is looked at, and can, in turn, return the look. That is why, for example, they did not call the face/mask of the Gorgon that way, because crossing their gaze, according to Greek mythology, was equivalent to death. And since it could not be looked at, it only had ahead, it did not prosopon. The same was true of the face of the dead since visual reciprocity with them was no longer possible. Well, in that community of face to face, the face does not conceal, or hide anything. On the contrary, it is a translucent film that expresses, reveals, and projects an outward-oriented personality. The same happens with the mask, which is more difficult for us to understand since we associate it with concealment; for the Greeks, on the other hand, it has mainly a function of representation and identification. Why?

The mask that was worn did not hide the face that was covered. It deleted and replaced it. Under the dramatic mask, the actor's face, replaced by sight, is abolished, and his own identity, the one that revealed his face, gives way to that of the character he embodies. He is now Hécuba, Príamo, or Paris.

Similarly, the faithful who participated in a ritual masquerade had no face other than their mask, and no other personality during the time of the ceremony.

To begin to think of the face and the mask as two different realities that can even be opposed, it is first necessary to distinguish them linguistically. This is what the Romans do: they call the mask a person, and the face is called a vultus or facies. The autonomy of these two notions (which is also expressed in Roman iconography) would allow them to think of them together or separately from now on, as we do. According to an old etymological tradition, the person would derive from the verb personal (that is, "to sound through something"); according to this explanation, the person would originally be the theatrical mask equipped with a special device that raised the voice of the actor. However, current etymologists prefer to root it in the Etruscan term phersu, which also meant 'mask.'

Person designates at the same time the mask and the role so that it does not indicate in the first place an individuality—whose representation would not need a mask—but a type, a timeless reality. But we found this semantic extension already in Greek, where, from s. II a. of C., prosopon comes to designate also a character (in Polibio, Plutarco, etc.). Also, prosopon begins to designate the "grammatical person": they would be something like "the faces put into play by the relation of the discourse" (the three Prosopis or persons of the discourse: me, you, him).

It is interesting to relate the notion of prosopon or person as 'character,' or 'role' with the evolution of the term character in Greek. Its initial meaning of "stamp," "mark," or "imprint" visible, acquired, between the 4th and 3rd centuries BC. C., the sense of "distinctive characteristic" and, finally, that of "moral character." According to the original sense, the character would be what is incised in the flesh or the soul in the manner of permanent writing. The 'characters' or dramatic personae find a symbolic representation in the masks of tragedy. These masks froze the expression in some emblematic configurations, recognizable even from a distance, thus creating an authentic expressive typology of the face. The rough man is depicted as having dark skin, eyes, and hair, with thick lips and warty nose; the noble-souled characters, the heroes, were generally represented with large-nosed "Greek-style" masks, etc. The playwright developed the physiognomic characterization, typifying the characters to the extreme. Each mask, as opposed to the others, emphasizing some somatic brand: "a kind of visual translation of what the encyclopedia of the time defined, on a semantic level, as a character, a passion, a vice or a virtue."

Thus, the character, the role referred to social types, not specifically to singular individuals. For a person to come to designate a new moral category, to end up meaning "every individual of the human species," many factors still have to come together: Roman law, Stoic ethics, and Christian theology have to be developed. It is the latter two that have brought us the notion of a moral person, while Roman law has left us that of a legal person.

Indeed, with Roman law, all free men of Rome become Roman citizens, all acquire a civilian person. That is, they become 'persons' capable of owning property, signing contracts, pleading, acquiring rights and contracting obligations, etc. In its fullness, only the paterfamilias will have that status. Of course, "servus non-habet personam" ("the slave has no person"), since the slave does not have ancestors and rights. Similarly, Greek jurisconsults call aprosoponslaves, who cannot represent themselves and are 'characterized' by their masters. Roman law, on the other hand, underlines the sense of role or social role given to "person": "homo plures personas substituent" ("man sustains many people"), which meant that "persona" is, in some way, a concept superimposed on that of man, since he is capable of 'supporting' or representing different functions, of putting on different 'masks': acting now as a father, now as a merchant, now as a faithful of such religion, etc.

But the notion of a person still lacks a clear metaphysical foundation, and Christianity is going to give it to them. As Mauss insists, it is then that "the transition from the notion of person, the man clothed in a state, to the notion of man without further ado, to that of the human person" will take place. That step begins to take shape, curiously, in the context of controversies about the unity of the Holy Trinity. In the S. IV, at the Council of Nicaea, theologians argue—in Greek—about the nature of Christ, and establish that he has a double nature (divine and human), but that he only has one person, who is unique and indivisible. Now the most commonly used Greek term for 'person' was not prosopon, but hypostasis, something like 'substrate' or 'substance.' A few decades later, Saint Augustine developed the notion of person, so that it could be used to refer to both the Trinity (the "three persons") and human beings. Furthermore, the idea of a person in Saint Augustine loses the relative exteriority that continued to characterize it, to focus decisively on.

But it was especially Boethius, in the 6th century, who gave the notion of person a definition that had a great following: "persona est naturae rationalis individua substantia" ("the person is an individual substance of a rational nature"). Person "would thus become the name of all the individuals of the human species, constituted by reason. So, the term, which had nothing metaphysical in origin, enters the vocabulary of ontology and ends up signifying the ultimate principle of individuation. In essence, it is what singularizes each one of us, and what singularizes us not accidentally, but substantially, what subsists or remains beyond of the changes and transformations. The Christian tradition spreads this notion that, later, is enriched by numerous thinkers with the notes of individuality, equality, immortality, dignity, transcendence, etc. Among them, Kant stands out, who highlights the ethical sense of "person" as "an end in itself, 'who' has dignity and no price. "

One of the most striking things about this etymological trajectory is that we move from an exterior and relational vision of the face/person to an interior and substantial one. As we have seen, in Greek antiquity, the prosopon, either as a face, as a mask or as a character, is something that is offered in the sight of others, which only makes sense in face to face. Also, in person, as a dramatic mask, as a character or as a role, or even in the legal entity in the vision of the first Roman law, we perceive that exteriority, that meaning only comprehensible in human intercommunication. In all these cases, these are representations and identifications that require alter egos, interlocutors, or spectators. On the other hand, in the metaphysical vision of the person as a substance (as the same word indicates, what underlies, what is below and is invariable, antithetical to our idea of the mask, as something superimposed, that hides), it is given an intrinsic value, a dignity of its own, independent of its social roles, its particular manifestations, and its masks.

In modern and contemporary times, however, many have reformulated a relational concept of the person, leaving aside its definition as "rational substance." Some of these modern trends take up the theatrical origin of a person to underline the character of human existence as Theatrum Mundi and of individuals as actors who play different roles in different situations, in the courts of justice or the rituals of society, no less than on stage. According to this perspective, our face would be a mask, or better, support for multiple masks, This is depending on the occasion, as in the sociological theory of E. Goffman, who popularizes the dramaturgical model to explain social interactions in which the self would not be more than a hanger where the dresses hang from the role she plays.

Thus, we would have gone from perceiving the masks as other faces, like the Greeks, to perceiving (in some cases) the faces as social masks. And now in the triple sense of representation, identification, and dissimulation. When we say of someone who "does not show his true face," who hides behind "a mask of hypocrisy," etc., we are not speaking as a Greek or as a member of a small community where communication is entirely face-to-face, where interiority and subjectivity have not been developed. We are speaking as modern subjects who perceive the face, at the same time, as a place of being and appearance, as a place of essence and pretense, of truth itself and artifice. The place where the soul shows and disguises itself. They wear masks, which they perceive according to those masks...

2. Portraits: the modern subject in their unique faces

Well, a brief history of modern portraiture leads us to explore, from another perspective, the complexity of the face/mask contrast that we have glimpsed in etymological history. What we generally call portraiture is the "representation of a subject" as it has developed—especially pictorially—from the 15th century to the 19th-century avant-garde. The idea that comes to mind first is that of similarity, that of mimesis: that the portrait constitutes a kind of frozen mirror, a permanent and generally improved reflection of the portrayed subject. For this reason, Peter Burke proposed this definition: "that representation of a person that his friends and relatives can recognize as his image, which includes from caricature at one end to idealization at the other."

But, in truth, a subject can be 'represented' without the exact physical resemblance being determining; whoever is presented with his name, or with a whole series of attributes or symbols corresponding to his position or his social position, already makes him 'recognizable.' In general, it is for this reason that we also speak of ancient, pre-Renaissance 'portraits' (and also of avant-garde and contemporary 'portraits'): because it is sufficient that the portrait evokes the person, even if it is not similar too. Furthermore, the essence of the portrait is not usually solely in its fidelity to the physical features of the model. In some way, he is expected to capture the interior of the model, the liveliness of his spirit, his truth. Every portrait thus aspires, in some way, to be a portrait of the soul or interiority. What is meant by interior or soul, here, is the question, because it is not the same as creating something singular (as "face") or as something typified (as "mask"), as a source of subjectivity or as the axis of social position. For this reason, the history of portraiture cannot but reflect the evolution of man's place in society, the evolution of ideas related to his value and dignity.

49

And it is fascinating to observe how this evolution is reflected in how man represents his image, his face.

It will be, therefore, the breeding ground of humanism of the Renaissance, the transition from a theocentric vision of life to an anthropocentric one, that makes the realistic figuration of people begin to be considered important and desirable. We will have to wait for the Flemish portrait of the 15th century (starting with van Eyck and van der Weyden) and the Italian and German portrait of the 16th (Dürer, Holbein, da Vinci, Rafael, Titian) for this decisive transformation and consolidation of the genre to begin. Pay off. Until then, it is normal to represent schematic types, sanctified forms of popes and kings, without the actual physical marks of individuation. Since the Renaissance, the portrait will remain largely a portrait of the power of the privileged; He will continue to try to impress and claim the recognition of the high status of the portrayed in society. But little by little, the number of people claiming for themselves that predominant social role will begin to expand. Thus, together with the princes and members of the high clergy and nobility, from the 16th century onwards, the bourgeois were also portrayed: merchants, bankers, artisans, humanists, and artists, thus contributing to enhancing their reputation.

Until the 16th century, "the physiognomy was not yet a showcase of character, the interior of the individual human being did not yet appear, but the external image of his social identity." Until then, the usual practice was to 'portray' the social masks (the prose of the leading actors in civil and religious life); Now, little by little, the individual will appear, he will go "from the painting of the name to the painting of the self" (Martínez-Artero 82). Indeed, it is almost commonplace—since Jacob Burckhardt already did it in The Culture of the Renaissance in Italy (1860)—to relate the emergence of portraiture at that time with the birth of individualism in the West. The existence of "galleries of illustrious men" to exalt the facts of outstanding individuals points to links between the rise of portraiture and what Burckhardt called "the modern sense of fame." It is also striking that the rise of self-portrait coincided with that of autobiography, or even that the literary portrait began to develop. That is, the narrative description of the faces of the characters, something unusual up to that time. Undoubtedly, the idea of an unrepeatable individual fits well with the increasing demands of plausibility, of the search for similarity. The life of painters Vasari's (1586) is symptomatic in this regard since he shows concern for the portraits and biographies of artists, two evident signs of the birth of individualism, of the appreciation of one's autonomy and individual freedom.

Although this individualistic society was only emerging timidly in the Renaissance, and the social role continued to be decisive (as corroborated, in turn, by multiple portraits), the truth is that this vision points to the most striking aspect developed by Western art. And especially for the portrait: its fundamental direction towards the subjective gaze and the singularizing and unique face of the portrayed subject. That this direction was not at all evident "is demonstrated by the fact that this has not happened in the other figurative traditions matured on this planet. Neither in Chinese, lyrical, and naturalistic painting. Nor in Byzantine, hieratic, transcendent, and spiritualist painting. Not in the Islamic, abstract, and irreverent. Not in the Indian, plastic, and decorative. Not in the African, synthetic, and in its formalistic way." According to Caroli, that approach of western figurative painting to individual psychology would constitute its main "originality."

The search for similarity that is an indication of this developing awareness of one's singularity did not exclude, in any case, a more or less high degree of idealization. As he explained, at the end of the 16th century, Lomazzo, in his painting treatise, "the painter, in the portrait, must always emphasize the dignity and greatness of the person and repress the imperfection of nature." Thus, many of the works of the Italian Renaissance—think of those of Boticelli, for example—as well as of the French painting of the time, looked like images of statues, rather than of flesh and blood beings: sharp figures, with smooth surfaces, wrinkle-free, perfectly silhouetted. In Flemish painting, which continues the line opened by Van Eyck, on the other hand, that is less common. Influenced, undoubtedly, due to the Protestant Reformation, the portrait began to function as a mirror that reflected the truth without beautifying touches; the figures begin to expose themselves to a clean face, often with all their ugliness. This is especially clear in the German, Flemish, and Dutch Mannerist and Baroque portraits.

Thus, psychological deepening reaches a more than remarkable virtuosity in baroque portraiture, with artists such as Velázquez, Rembrandt, Franz Hals, Rubens, or Goya. The portrait becomes more stark and realistic, often without idealization. Also, the list of people portrayed will be increasing, since although the portraits of royalty and bourgeois portraits commissioned are the main ones, some painters will start to notice the others, in the miserable, the mentally disabled, the humble. Note that until then they had not appeared reflected in the artistic works. But "as it had already happened with the painting of the mad, elderly, blind, crippled and physically handicapped in general who had invaded the art of Brueghel and Bosco, the Renaissance images of the poor did not constitute true individual portraits, but rather showed almost caricatural human types, charged in addition to moral connotations." They were the representation of vice and unreason rather than that of a specific dispossessed. But, already at the beginning of the 17th century, Annibale Carracci, Caravaggio, Ribera, Murillo, and other artists made what appear to be true portraits of humble figures such as a water carrier or a street egg fryer. However, yes, they were still anonymous figures, their names did not matter. In the 18th century, painters like Traversi, Chardin, or Goya also portrayed other humble figures, not as mere funny characters or as representatives of any profession, but as individuals with their faces. The neoclassical and romantic portraits (David, Ingres, Delacroix), however, once again gave greater idealization to the characters, to the detriment of the realism achieved in the previous stages. Velázquez painted the dwarves and jesters of the court, endowing them with considerable dignity.

With the avant-garde begins the decline of what until then had been understood as a portrait. From 1900, mimesis, the resemblance of the artistic portrait with the one portrayed is no longer a defining criterion. So in these cases, we can only continue to speak of portraits in an approximate sense, by evocation. Therefore, there is talk of the decline of the portrait genre. Now, we must be clear that we are speaking from an artistic point of view since from a sociological point of view, one cannot speak of failure, but the absolute triumph of the portrait after the invention of photography and the subsequent techniques of visual reproduction. It cannot be denied that quantitatively speaking, this is the contemporary, the true golden age of portraiture. So much that, we can speak of the "triumph-defeat", "of the contemporary portrait": the portrait as a mere document overwhelmingly triumphs; portrait as art suffers a defeat or, at least, an overwhelming transformation.

Photography, invented by Niepce in 1824, and perfected by Daguerre, came into the public domain from 1839. By then the commissioned pictorial portrait had already reached, since the second half of the 18th century, an unprecedented extension. The demand to have your image, the awareness of your uniqueness, will only grow dramatically in increasingly larger layers of society through the photographic technique, a more comfortable, economical, and exact way of accessing reproduction. The invention of photography coincides, moreover, with an industrial revolution that profoundly modifies local belongings, provokes the rural exodus, accentuates urbanization, and arouses in more and more people the feeling of their individuality. It is significant. Seeing oneself, therefore, becomes a constant, almost banal fact. And more with photography, which supposes, even more, this "advent of myself as another," in the words of Roland Barthes: "[t] he curious that the disorder (of civilization) that this new act announces has not been thought of. " Without a doubt, already at the end of the XIX century, we are in the process of democratizing individualism.

Precisely, owning your image, a singularizing portrait, ceases to be a distinctive sign, a privilege of a few. The opportunity to have a face that provides anyone with a photographic portrait irritates more than one, beginning with Baudelaire, who—in 1859—writes: "[a] filthy society rushes like a single Narcissus to contemplate his trivial image on the metal. A few years earlier, in 1850,

Melville had already expressed his deep displeasure: "the portrait, instead of immortalizing the genius as it did before, will do little more than show a fool to the taste of fashion. And when everyone disposes of his portrait, the true distinction will undoubtedly consist of having none."

Melville, undoubtedly, failed to understand what was coming: the absolute impossibility in a world like ours of staying aniconic, of withdrawing from having multiple portraits and images of ourselves. Sooner rather than later, in the second half of the 19th century, various proposals began to be considered to establish an identification document with a photograph of the face. At the Universal Exposition of 1867, in Paris, they were already used as access letters. Later, the police authorities and the state administration would soon develop the idea. In essence, each individual should be identified using an identification letter with his full name and a photograph of his face. A photograph from the front, with the most neutral expression possible, without a smile or gesture of any kind. Exactly like the photo of the National Identity Document that every five or ten years, we must renew, face resting on a light background. Made mechanically, often without human mediation (in a practical photo booth), we tend to call it a "passport photo" since we are no longer even aware that we are making a portrait. A portrait that long ago became mandatory as an identifying document.

Painting could hardly rival the hyperrealism that photography produced. It is clear that what was once interpreted as stiff competition, was also liberating for the plastic arts. The obsession with mimesis, with perfect resemblance, decreased— that was what photography was for; the artist was free to explore abstract pathways, beyond the formal imitation of nature. This, as it could not be otherwise, greatly affected the most symbolic of genres: the portrait.

3. The "defeat of the face"?

Thus, begins with the avant-gardes—and especially with cubism—a process of disfigurement, of progressive loss of the degree of similarity that scandalized the spectators of its time. Suddenly, the portrayed subject tends to blur, to merge with the other elements of the environment. Without meatiness, the faces flatten out, become uniform. For Galienne and Pierre Francastel, it is no longer possible to speak of portraiture, given that— following the path inaugurated by Cézanne— artists consider subjects as fragments of reality among other fragments:

It is a portrait when an artist simply uses the features of a face to introduce them into a composition that in his eyes has another purpose. But only when, in his spirit, the real purpose of the work done is to interest us by the figure of the model by itself. Now, at no time does a Matisse or a Picasso try to link us to the personality of their model. They only insert him into the complex network of his imaginary activities.

In other words:

Fauves and Cubists use man as they do with a bottle or a guitar, as a simple accident of the sensible, without granting any action to the individual character of this object. Nor to the possibility that it embodies something different from themselves.

However, it is not only in portraits, but in representations of heads and faces in general, where this disfigurement occurs, to such an extent that there are those, like Jacques Aumont, who speak of a "defeat of the face" that would be appreciated evidently in avant-garde painting. And which is later extended to all parts of the image society: from the cinema to the press, from advertising to television. This "defeat" would be expressed in factors such as the following:

Return of the type, of the generic: the individual only interests insofar as he belongs to a class or a group; the representation of the face excludes the expression or only includes it if it strengthens the type, the trans individual. The extent of roughness: [...] reaches everything, potentially—animals, masks, landscapes, parts of the face. The disintegration of the face, rejection of its unity: parts of the face cut out, glued, returned to the surface of the image. Infinite magnification, monstrosity of the size, or sometimes, on the contrary, lilliputization. All kinds of damages, erasures, tears.

Factors, all of them, that would abound in the same direction: "that of an abandonment of the reference to the face as an expressive concentrate of humanity. And even, in most cases, that of deliberate destruction of that reference.

All these movements of disfigurement, of decomposition, are perceived, indeed, in contemporary painting: exploded faces (by the cubism of Braque or Picasso); scattered faces (scattered all over the canvas, Duchamp; and more, with the collage technique); twisted faces (faces like rubber; or bitten, gnawed on the inside ..., Francis Bacon); crossed out faces (scraped, as with wounds ..., Atlan, Dubuffet, Lam); unfocused faces (frequent in the 70s in paintings made from photographs ..., Gerhard Richter); enlarged faces (Warhol and pop art, Chuck Close ...), etc.

We could easily increase the list since there are very many cases in which the subjectivity of the portrayed individual is diluted, turned into one more of an anonymous mass. As there are numerous portraits in which the face resembles a mask.

Consider the famous portrait of Gertrude Stein, painted by Picasso in 1906: his face is like a wood carving, smooth and impersonal without any accident. Even clearer in Matisse's 'portrait' of Ivonne Landsberg, strikingly similar to an African mask. Something similar occurs in portraits painted by Modigliani or Giacometti, for example. These "portraits" are hardly distinguishable from the other paintings of anonymous and depersonalized faces that appear in the paintings of avant-garde artists. Malevitch, for example, approaches the art of icons: his flat, geometric, austere pictures, present frontal characters, a kind of mannequins or robots, immobile, timeless, with empty faces and erased features. Sometimes he replaces the features of their faces with the hammer and sickle, other times with the Christian cross. Like the Chirico mannequins, those egg-shaped heads, which cannot look at, nor be distinguished by unique features, have no individualizing signs, they are just pawns of the mass, expressionless machines.

Many other artistic portraits of the twentieth century, driven by German expressionism (think of the portraits of Kirchner, Beckman, or Otto Dix), lose the calm of the factions at rest, as until then had been customary, and add the cry, the disfigurement conscious, violence. In addition to this, it is not often a single portrait (portrait-summary or portrait-biography) of the model, but a series of them, often following a process of metamorphosis. The classical genre of portraiture was based on the idea that the identity of an individual was fundamentally defined and more or less invariable so that the portraitist only had to capture it on the canvas, copying his features, the expression of his character. The artist of the 20th century, on the other hand, has often repeatedly portrayed the same person, each time with a different identity, refractory to the idea that only one of them is the 'true' one. In this sense, some conceive the genre of modern portraiture as "a sample of masks—as, perhaps, all portraits to a certain extent—but differently insofar as it is openly and consciously."

Also, Warhol's 'portraits' are more like a mask or a surface without substance, without any psychological background. As numerous critics have pointed out, rather than making portraits, Warhol fabricated icons transforming the identity of his characters—and himself—into a frozen and depersonalized image through the manipulation of photography. With that brilliant use of superficiality, he is considered the perfect illustrator of show society, the initiator of postmodern aesthetics that today floods advertising in all its forms everywhere.

In recent decades there has been talking of a boost in portraiture, especially after the revitalization of the English figurative school, with Hockney, Freud, and Bacon. Undoubtedly, a renewed attempt to unravel man is perceived in them. Lucian Freud, for example, develops the tendency (rare in the classical portrait era) to portray his characters (and himself) completely nude, making the whole body, and not just the face, a significant psychological canvas. Francis Bacon also focuses obsessively on the human bodies he 'portrays': beings always isolated, helpless, unstable, whose bodily and facial limits are unfinished, blurred, or rather twisted, outlined, deformed. It is in many of his works of contorted, mutilated bodies, with broken or half-erased faces, which express—and create in the viewer—considerable existential anguish. Cortés affirms: "[n]o there is no identity, only pain, animal rebellion, threatened mortal flesh" and he adds: "what Bacon tries to capture is the psyche of the subject, his determined efforts to get to know him and to define himself in an image that spreads and disperses as a response to the myth of the subject's unity.

The "myth of the unity of the subject": this is precisely what seems to have been blown to pieces in the contemporary era. Pedro Azara interprets that setback of the traditional portrait (which captured that whole subject so serenely and recognizably) as a consequence of the death (disappearance or concealment) of God, so often proclaimed since the 19th century. If we were made in his image and likeness, and now it no longer exists, it is that we no longer have a model, an image to resemble and according to which to compose our integrity. The disappearance of God also entails the loss of faith in the unity of being. So only appearances would remain: "the contemporary artist is content with masks because the model no longer exists (outside of the mask game)." This fact would not stop revealing the condition of the current man:

The image, which in ancient times had the purpose of rescuing the soul from death and oblivion, giving them back an imperishable body, has ended up being the exposition of the fleeting and terminal condition of contemporary man.

But it is in the multiform society of the image where the most fundamental manifestations of the "defeat of the face" would be appreciated, according to Jacques Aumont. The symptoms of this 'defeat' that we have seen in pictorial art, or those that Aumont himself analyzes in the recent history of cinema, would only be reflections of the more general decomposition of the face in the extra-artistic circulation of images. His thesis is that "representation has extremely affected his most beloved object": "by dint of being the target of gazes, the face is disfigured." If in the early days of the naturalistic representation of the face, it obeyed a humanistic impulse to dignify man (at least the one portrayed), the main effect of all this would be, therefore, the preeminence of the type of the generic face removed from its individuality. A process that began in the early days of the technical reproduction of the face, with the beginning of photography as a documentary medium that leaves the multiple faces that it depicts anonymous or, moreover, contributes to catalogs, typologies, supporting the administrative and police eagerness: "[t] he faces must be identical, not to the subject, but its definition. It is no longer the window of the soul, but a poster, a slogan, a label".

The largest means of diffusion of faces today, television, which constantly accompanies us with its talking busts and close-ups, and where we see millions of faces, near and far, nominated or unnamed, parades, produces an effect of massification, saturation. And, of course, being the basic pillar of the image society, it is full of advertising, direct—more usual—indirect, which refers to some typology, to a succession of stereotypical features and gestures. The faces of the advertising are faces that represent an ideal of the consumer/spectator, and that they are generally of an exalted perfection, fruit of the computer retouching. Bottomless perfection, like the mannequin in a shop window. And it is that in the face of the advertising, the portrait we will hardly find the soul. Rather, we will only be left with the suspicion that there is nothing underneath that beautiful facade. These stylized advertising portraits are nothing more than mock portraits, brand masks that they promote.

In short, has this overexploitation of the image and its technical reproduction means become today a factor of trivialization, depriving the face of the meaning and value that its first humanistic representations seemed to confer on it? Does the hypertrophy of the face or its representation suppose its loss, its silence, its dissolution in the mass?

4. Individualism and mass society: faces and masks

We have seen it in the brief tours of the etymological history and the history of the portrait. For a long time, the gregarious conformation of social groups did not raise concern in their contemporaries for their faces; the singularity was not valued, the feeling of autonomy or personal freedom was not associated with the social definition of the individual. It is in modernity when there is a sharper awareness of man's individuality, a 'feeling of self' that accompanies—and is enhanced by—the diffusion of the mirror and the portrait in which the singular similarity of the model is sought. The face is beginning to be valued as an element of individuation and an exponent of human dignity, in parallel with the rise of individualism in privileged social classes.

As the anthropologist and sociologist David Le Breton emphasizes:

The promotion of the individual on the scene of history is contemporary with the acute feeling that he has a body and the dignity of a face that reveals before everyone's eyes at the same time his humanity and his dissimilarity.

There is no doubt that—Le Breton continues—"the more importance society gives to individuality, the more the value of the face will increase [since, ultimately, the dignity of the individual implies that of the face]." In all this process, it seems clear, therefore, that the singularity of the face calls for the singularity of man as a person.

The visualization, objectification, and externalization of one's face and that of others is positive to promote that self-awareness. At the end of the 19th century, the proliferation of useful artifacts for this purpose (mirror, photography, pictorial portrait), coincided in the West with the industrialization, urbanization and growing uprooting of holistic societies, which extended to large layers of the population. That awareness of one's individuality. It was this same process that led to the mass society, and eminently urban society, with a multiplied population.

The first great thinkers of this modern technological metropolis—like Simmel, Spengler, Kracauer, Jünger, or Benjamin, however already warned about the dissolution of the modern individual in the massification and gregariousness of big cities. All of them alluded in one way or another to the neutralization of the face in the anonymity of the mass; they spoke of the masks that would populate that metropolitan universe, deprived of individual expressiveness. And it is that the development of medicine, hygiene, education, the migration of the population, contributed more and more to the homogenization of physical types and to erase in the constitution of the citizen middle classes the social origins inscribed on their faces. The identity of origin is blurred, the faces, the clothes, the gaits begin to homogenize, to become anonymous. The reflex mechanisms of imitation and collective emulation of behavior, as well as gestures and facial expressiveness, promote a massive resemblance.

The homogenization and typification of the forms would come hand in hand, of course, to standardization and neutralization of the characters, to a depersonalization of the individual. In several of the cited authors, the mass-man, cannon fodder of the totalitarianism of both signs, is already foreshadowed. The very dissolution or alienation of the face in much of 20th-century art—which we have reviewed—can also be understood as an attempt to capture that social reality: the face of crowds, an empty, interchangeable, anonymous stain. Or erased, devoid of singularity.

In that sense, all those thinkers already announced, in some way, the "defeat of the face" that we read in Jacques Aumont. That technician mass society and, later, that image and consumer society, would have privileged the technical-objective-conceptual gaze that transforms quality into quantity, the face into the number, into a stereotype; in short, in a mask. Role theories to explain our social interactions also start from this principle: they announce that in those interactions, we deal with masks—classes of masks, stereotypes, like those personae Roman—more than with singular, unique faces. The mask determines who I deal with and what my responses should be; that is, social learning would consist largely of assimilating the meanings of each tip or mask and displaying the associated responses.

Now, the affirmation that our social interaction is a relation of the masks already had its most radical prophet in Nietzsche. For him, the logic of the mask leads to the annihilation of the face: there is no longer an interiority to hide. It speaks of the multiplicity of masks that we wear so that the subject would be nothing but their masks, without behind, underneath, within each one of them there is an I, a character, an individual, but only another and another mask, up to Infinity. It would be, therefore, the realm of pure appearance devoid of essence.

But, if this were the case, the very idea of a mask would lose its meaning, since the idea of artificially concealing, hiding, or covering something remains implicit in it: a natural, authentic, substantial face against the variability of the mask. That is, the interior/exterior, essence/appearance dichotomies would no longer make sense as such. And this would suppose a metaphysical revolt that, however much one may think in the philosophical field, exceeds our common life.

In front of the spokesmen of the "defeat of the face," who affirm things such as that "the long historical period of full characters and real faces has passed, absorbed by the ageless history of empty masks and faces virtual, I am inclined to think that contemporary, urban, media and mass society offers both the opportunity to dignify and typify the face. That is to say, the contemporary society of the image reproduces to the end the two faces of which we spoke before: to a great extent, of course, the social mask, the typology, the assignment of individuals to some groups, according to stereotypes; but also the individual face, the one that was the protagonist of the classic portrait, the one to whom all the depths of the soul dance in the face, and the valuable singularity of their emotions and thoughts. The media preponderance of the first face may not be enough to talk about his "defeat," as Aumont does, nor to maintain that all interaction is a relationship between masks; no, at least, as long as the humanist causes that the other face continues to battle, while we continue to remember or enhance the meaning and value of that face.

CHAPTER 6

PSYCHOLOGICAL WARFARE

Psychological Warfare is used to influence the opinion, feelings, attitude, and behavior of the enemy. Be they people, allied and neutral nations, or the masses under the control of the enemy. So that they support the objectives and achievements of the mission entrusted by the one who employs it.

The Psychological War tries to change the mentality of the masses that support the enemy forces through propaganda systems.

Concept

Psychological warfare, or war without rifles, is the planned use of propaganda and psychological action aimed at directing behavior, in pursuit of objectives of social, political, or military control, without resorting to the use of weapons.

The concept of war of nerves is synonymous with the war of Zappa, terminology used by San Martín, one of the creators of modern psychological warfare.

Description

Psychological warfare consists of scaring the enemy to reduce their chances of success in combat. Psychological warfare seeks, on the one hand, to paralyze the adversary, to defeat him before he even enters to fight, and, on the other hand, to win the "minds and hearts" of the people he does not intend to demolish.

Experts on the matter believe that war is not won only in the trenches, or from the air with refined and sophisticated automated weapon systems. But it can be won, also, in the minds of people, both from their side and from the enemy.

Psychological Operations

Psychological Operations, also known by its acronym (OPSIC), is a term that replaced that of psychological warfare in 1957, (although currently used simultaneously). It has planned actions to transmit information and selective signals to foreign audiences and influence their emotions, motivations, reasoning and finally the behavior of governments, organizations, groups, and individuals.

It is the set of persuasive measures in times of peace or war that are designed to influence the attitudes, opinions, and behavior of the opposing forces, be they civilian or military, to achieve national objectives.

The purpose of psychological operations is aimed at inducing or reinforcing in foreign audiences the attitudes and behaviors favorable to the objectives from which they originated.

Psychological warfare and psychological operations have also been known under other terms, such as political warfare, to "win minds and hearts."

The term psychological warfare is used to "define any action that is practiced primarily by psychological methods to evoke a planned psychological reaction for other people."

Various techniques are used to carry it out, and it is aimed at influencing the value system, belief system, emotions, reasoning, or public behavior.

This is used to elicit confessions or affirm beneficial beliefs and actions to the person who has a particular intent. They are also paired with covert operations and false flag tactics.

This is often used to break enemy morale using techniques that help weaken state troops.

The targets can be governments, organizations, groups, and individuals, and not just soldiers. Civilians from foreign countries may also be the targets, with the use of new technologies and the media, to cause some effect on the government of that country.

Psychological warfare procedures

Among the various procedures, methods, and tactics used are:

1) The Letters

They are written in personal form or by pseudonyms, having as content facts and incidents manufactured to align, scandalize, create conflicts, and arouse suspicions within the adversary to seek a psychological transformation.

It is one of the best means of Psychological Warfare, due to its economic simplicity and the major effects it causes.

2) The Slogans

They are short words or phrases that are a vivid and powerful statement to express ideas, inspire the psychological requirements of the masses, and to seek the psychological transformation of adverse organizations. They must have the following characteristics:

a) Current validity responding to the situation.
b) It must tend towards the strengthening of the National Policy.
c) Satisfy the wishes of the people; for example, the slogan of the French Revolution "Liberty or Death."
d) It must stimulate and encourage; for example: "I'd rather die fighting than ..." or "I have sacred duties ...".
e) They must attack the main target.

3) The Rumors

They are unfounded words that circulate in society, and that, applied in the Psychological War, have functions to discourage, confuse, and alter order within the opponent.

They take advantage of the psychological factors of the people, such as curiosity, suspicion, desire, horror, and hatred.

Nowadays

Currently, the "power of the media" is often a recurring theme, as they install debate topics, ideas about the "good and the bad," define presidential elections and impose certain consumptions.

However, very little is said about psychological warfare. Below, we present a brief historical review that is essential to understand how and why psychological warfare strategies continue to be applied today, which seem to continue the Cold War in the region.

In general, psychological warfare is understood as propaganda and deception through the media.

However, it is something much broader, considering the practices implemented since its institutionalization (early Cold War) until today. It includes and combines development assistance strategies (economic pressure and extortion), handling of information, propaganda, cultural and educational programs, student exchange, training of leaders and security, military intervention, and generally low intensity.

It is a war that combines political, economic, cultural, and military aspects. People's psychological factors, such as curiosity, suspicion, desire, horror, and hatred, are exploited.

Influential aspects for its application:

- Appropriate opportunities to spread rumors.

- It takes into account when major changes or disorders occur in the adverse ranks of the organization, or possibilities of its occurrence arise.
- When there is discontent or confusion in the masses controlled by the adversaries.
- When their leaders have been captured or attacked, ideological disorientation reigning in their cadres.
- When they are in disorderly retreat or when the opponent is cornered.

Principles for creating rumors:

-Adapting to the desire or mental state of the target:

- Attack the opponent's weaknesses based on his mental state.
- Exaggerate minor facts and vice versa.
- They must be based on important, strange, and curious aspects that concern everyone.
- Using infiltrators to spread the rumors, so that their effects are greater.

Example of Psychological Warfare

One of the paradigmatic cases of this war is the one directed against the governments of Hugo Chávez and Nicolás Maduro in Venezuela. Although it seems simple and repeated, oil is undoubtedly the axis of this conflict, since it is a fundamental resource for the reproduction of the United States' military-industrial complex.

The Bible refers to various events that occurred in antiquity, and among them, the case of Gideon stands out. This biblical character excluded 25,000 soldiers from the 40,000 he had to select to join his army. This happened because his men confessed, after a series of interrogations, that they were afraid of the fight. Thus, he made a psychological selection.

In the writings of the Chinese strategist Sun Tzu Sun, vestiges of psychological warfare can be found, as he set out to subjugate his enemy "without firing a shot."

Another example can be found in the famous boast of Genghis Khan (the Mongol general Temujin), who weakened the enemy's combative will by spreading rumors about the strength and ferocity of his army. His planning was simple, outstanding, and effective.

The concept of war of nerves is synonymous with the war of Zappa, which was the terminology used by San Martín (I), one of the creators of modern psychological warfare. San Martín, in Peru, exclusively managed the psychological factor. In this way, he was able to get to Lima without firing a single shot and with the loss of very few men, recorded in isolated and extremely minor combats.

During World War I, psychological operations became formal. Almost all the countries involved in the war used some form of propaganda in their strategies and tactics, and most of them organized specialized military units in that activity.

Propaganda activities began to be known as "psychological operations" or Psychological Warfare during World War II.

Application by the United States

As it is known, it was in the Korean War (1950 - 1953), where for the first time, the US in an orderly and planned manner used the Psychological War as part of the warlike actions in the military conflict.

It was a few years before that the US Armed Forces (1949) developed their first regulation for the conduct of psychological operations (OP).

To carry out the PO in Korea, an apparatus and a structure were created with the necessary units. In 1951, the US Department of Defense created a Psychological Warfare Directorate, also organizing the system for preparing cadres and specialists for the new structure created. For the year 1952, the Psychological Warfare Center was located in Fort Bragg (State of North Carolina).

At the end of the Korean War, the US Armed Forces unified the GP apparatus with that of the Special Forces, leaving the Psychological Operations (OP) as part of the Special Operations (OE).

As of this moment, there has been no attempted coup d'état, military intervention, "humanitarian" intervention, or US intervention, in which the Special Operations and Psychological Warfare Forces have not been involved.

Relationship with Informative War

In recent times the term Information Warfare has been positioning itself in the slang of analysts, who in one way or another study and investigate these processes. It is no secret to anyone that after the collapse of the socialist camp and the repositioning of parties and left movements in the world, the language of war prevails in the international arena. Yugoslavia, Afghanistan, Iraq, Sudan, Rwanda, Somalia, Libya, Haiti, [[Honduras], Bosnia-Herzegovina and currently Syria, Iran, North Korea, Venezuela and the never forgotten Cuba are examples of this.

Beyond the military context

This proposal is not exclusive to military confrontations, as it is also present in other types of situations. There are wars of this nature between couples undergoing separation, between companies vying for the same niche or between mass communication.

How to Enter Your Clients' Mind

Human behavior does not very much. This is why salespeople and marketing teams have been using psychology as a tool to get more customers, creating loyalty in them, and ultimately their most precious goal: sales. It is not necessary to give examples, and it is enough to pay a little attention to online advertisements, on television, in magazines, on the street, etc. If they use psychology, it is basically because it works.

Therefore, these techniques can also be applied to social networks. Let's see here some of the most successful strategies:

1. Giving gifts

Giving gifts to users generates a kind of commitment to correspond later with the company.

When you are given a gift, the first two thoughts that probably come to mind are: say thank you and "in return, I have to do something for this person."

The gifts you offer need not be extravagant or expensive. Here are some examples of attractive gifts that are easy to give and will encourage your users to become customers:

- A discount or extra money on next purchase in exchange for subscribing to your mailing list.
- An extension of an offer for a few days, in exchange for sharing images of the product or service received on social networks.
- A low-cost gift item included in a purchase order.
- A free electronic book.

2. Don't give too many options

If you give people too many options, they can feel overwhelmed.

Decision making is a stressful process and can harm a person's mood; The result may be that your potential customer "bounces" and leaves before making a purchase. Instead, creating a limited number of options makes choices easier to make. There may be cases where offering only a single option is the best thing to do.

3. Become an expert

Before consumers shop, they seek advice and opinions from others they feel they can trust. This could mean that they are going to check web pages to read people's opinions about products and services. Therefore, they will visit forums, sites, and social networks to investigate. Fortunately, you can also become their source of information. Create a blog with interesting articles and lots of useful content about your products and services and related topics that can add knowledge to your customers.

4. Add emotion to the equation

Every time you enter Facebook, you will see at least one video or meme that appeals to emotion or makes you feel passionate about something. This is because emotional content has a big impact. It is attractive, and people tend to like and share this type of post.

Does it mean that sharing self-improvement videos and pets in funny situations will increase your website traffic or that sales will go up? No, not necessarily; However, what should be clear is the importance of the emotional impact of your content.

5. Make your users feel part of your company

Social media marketing is about building relationships. Your goal is to create an online social circle that spans all social media platforms so that people want to become a part of that circle, and then make them feel valued when they arrive.

This can be done with simple actions like posting a thank you message when you are followed on Twitter or responding to comments on Facebook. You can even take this a step further by finding followers who are providing you with a great deal of engagement and reaching out to them as a hobby and sharing your content. This can not only build brand loyalty, it could even lead to them becoming ambassadors for your brand.

5 Techniques to Read People

Cold reading is an analytical and communication tool between individuals increasingly used in professional communication. It makes it possible to target the needs of a person quickly, to communicate effectively. It makes it possible to recover information on an individual by observing his reactions and an imprecise line of questioning to target his needs or his shortcomings quickly.

It is used by sellers, interrogators, psychologists, politicians, hypnotists, magicians, seers, mentalists, palmists, astrologers, sects, and scammers. Knowing your techniques well is an effective way to better communicate with your loved ones, but also a way to protect yourself from manipulation better.

1. Watch the signals of body language

Research has shown that words make up only 7% of how we communicate, while body language (55%) and tone of voice (30%) make up the rest.

Reading non-verbal language is divided into three main categories:

Observe the posture: When you read the posture of people, ask yourself the question: Do they have their heads held high, self-confidence? Or are they walking indecisively or curled up, a sign of low self-esteem? Do they strut around with a swollen chest, a sign of a big ego?

Observe the physical movements: Are they leaning towards us or not? In general, we lean towards those we love, and we move away from those we do not love. Do they cross their legs and arms? This often suggests a defensive attitude, anger, or self-protection. In what direction are the feet pointing? In general, the feet point towards the person with whom they are most comfortable. Are the hands hidden? When people put their hands under their knees, in their pockets or behind their back, it suggests that they are hiding something.

Observe the facial expression: Emotions can be engraved on our faces. The deep wrinkles in the face suggest excessive worry or thinking. Crow's feet are the smile lines of joy. Pursed lips signal anger, contempt, or bitterness. A tight jaw and gnashing of teeth are signs of tension.

To go further and become a real pro of nonverbal language, I highly recommend the training *The Basics of Nonverbal Communication* by Annabelle Boyer, an expert in non-verbal language and human behavior.

2. Pay attention to the appearance

We can learn a lot about people's personalities by simply looking at their appearance. Do they wear a power suit and well-waxed shoes, dressed for success, indicating ambition? Jeans and a T-shirt, indicating that they are comfortable with relaxation? A tight top with a neckline, indicating the desire to seduce? A pendant such as a cross or a Buddha indicating spiritual values?

3. Watch your breath

"I feel like I can't breathe, like I'm sinking."

How does he breathe? If someone is breathing from the chest, it means they are relaxed. If his breathing is shallow, then he is tense. If you want to know someone's mental state, watch their breath.

If his breathing is choppy, he will be more likely to be nervous, which means there is something he doesn't want you to know. The reason may be shyness, anxiety, or that he is hiding something from you. If someone is breathing from their stomach, then you know that their mental state is calm, which generally means that they are sincere.

4. Trust your intuition

Intuition is what your gut feels, not what your head says. It is non-verbal information that you perceive through sensations, rather than your logic. Listen to what your instincts tell you, especially during the first meetings.

Here are three techniques to better understand your intuition:

Your visceral reactions: Visceral reactions occur before you have had time to think and manifest yourself quickly since it is a primary biological reaction. They tell you whether you are comfortable or not, and they are your internal truth barometer, which lets you know if you can trust people.

Goosebumps: Goosebumps are a wonderful part of intuition that makes us understand that we are in resonance with the people who touch us, inspire us, or tell us something that touches a sensitive chord. Goosebumps also occur when you experience deja-vu, a recognition that you have known someone before, even if you have never met them.

Intuitive empathy: Sometimes, you can feel the physical symptoms and emotions of the people in your body, which is an intense form of empathy. Does my back hurt when it didn't hurt before? Am I depressed or upset after an uneventful meeting?

5. Perceive the emotional energy

Emotions are an amazing expression of our energy and the "vibe" we give off. We record them with our intuition. Having people you feel good with improves your mood and vitality. Other people are exhausting, you have low energy, and you instinctively want to get away.

Here are four techniques for reading emotional energy:

Feel the presence of people: It is the global energy that we emit, which does not necessarily correspond to words or behaviors. It is the emotional atmosphere that surrounds us like a cloud of rain or the sun. Do they have a friendly presence that attracts you? Where do you get goosebumps, making you back off?

Notice the feeling of a handshake, a hug, and a touch: We share our emotional energy through physical contact, much like an electric current. Ask yourself: is a handshake or hug warm, comfortable, confident? Or is it off-putting, so you want to retire?

Listen to the tone of the voice: The tone and volume of our voice can speak volumes about our emotions. Sound frequencies create vibrations. When you read people, notice how the tone of their voice affects you. Ask yourself: Is the tone of their voice soothing? Or is it abrasive, snarling, or whiny?

Look at people's eyes: Our eyes transmit powerful energy. Just as the brain has an electromagnetic signal that extends beyond the body, studies indicate that the eyes also project it. Take the time to observe people's eyes. Are they attentive? Sexy? Quiet? Bad guys? Angry?

CHAPTER 7

BEHAVIORAL AND CHARACTER TRAITS OF MANIPULATORS

Shake Your Confidence

Self-confidence means being sure of our worth, capacity and strength, regardless of the situation we are in. Someone who is self-confident has a good sense of self-worth and self-awareness—expressing calmness, serenity, and self-confidence. Trust in oneself is also related to possessing some expertise and abilities, whether learned or innate.

Although possessing aptitude in a particular field will help increase self-esteem, self-confidence is not a prerequisite. Someone will get positive self-esteem without any pressure.

How to bolster self-confidence: Conditioning

The first step to create a sense of self-confidence is conditioning. It is extrinsic, that is, an outward strategy, in which action is taken to inspire trust in oneself. This is the most common approach within the culture of self-help, and also the best way to produce results. For example, an exercise in self-confidence is based on making an optimistic phrase, believing you already have a certain height, positively speaking and behaving, etc.

Here are few examples of how to use training to:

- Improve self-esteem: clothing: dress elegantly, have a good look and a healthy presentation
- Body language: walking and speaking have a purpose, be cool and composed, hold your head straight, maintain a good attitude and smile
- Motivational techniques: positive thinking, visualizing positive outcomes/scenarios, concentrate on strengths rather than flaws.

These actions are useful because they can provide a confidence boost almost immediately after taking them. However, the effects are seldom lasting; that is, you need to remind yourself to do them repeatedly. Otherwise, the results will dissipate over time.

Tips to shake your confidence

The second is to work on the issues that make you feel low in self-confidence. This is the most practical approach to shake your confidence.

Acquisition of symbols of value

Self-confidence is often linked to possessing certain knowledge, abilities, and skills. There is a lack of trust in many people because they believe they lack a certain skill. For example, if you don't feel confident about your role in a job, it may be because you lack the information and knowledge necessary to perform well. People with a high level of competence in a certain area often develop great self-confidence in that area as a result.

Competence can always be developed through reading and practice. For example, if you play sports and are preparing for a competition, you should train every day. Whether it's a presentation or public speaking, continually practice in front of different audiences to develop your skills. Eventually, you will find yourself so competent in that area that you will feel naturally confident in it.

In addition to the competition, there are other symbols of value, of which the most common are:

- Attributes such as the level of attractiveness, popularity, grace...
- Material possessions such as the amount of wealth you own, cars, property, luxury brands, etc.

- Status symbols such as academic qualifications, achievements, job
- Depending on the value symbol that is relevant to you, you can purchase it to increase self-confidence. For example, throughout life, different people pursue different things to increase their sense of self-esteem. Some people strive to be more attractive and popular. Some people try to acquire material possessions, such as making more money and buying material goods. Others seek to obtain status symbols and titles.

The problem with acquiring symbols of value to shake your confidence is that the increase in self-confidence only lasts as long as the symbols are valid. If they lose their relevance as a symbol of value, self-confidence will change accordingly.

Therefore, to increase your self-confidence permanently and in the long term, there is another option.

Projecting the Blame

The unconscious guilt that is deeply in our subconscious is not guilt that comes from any personal history, that you feel guilty for something you have done, but it is guilt without reason. It is a feeling of deep emptiness present in all conditions. This deep-rooted guilt makes us judge absolutely everything that happens, including ourselves as the protagonist of the story. This guilt comes from the belief in separation, and this belief in guilt always asks for punishment.

Punishment represents different ways to attack myself unconsciously. The ego uses other people and myself through illness, feeling unwell, etc. in my own body to prove that I have sinned.

Take a moment to reflect on your life and make a list of some ways the ego uses your body, or others to prove your guilt.

Any painful sensation that we experience in the body include anxiety, confusion, weight gain, devaluation, low self-esteem, illness, scarcity, physical or emotional pain, depression, conflict, anger, etc. We can stop judging them and learn to look at them. Realize that any painful symptoms we experience are a form of punishment and a consequence, and the true cause is our unforgiven belief in sin. Sin begets guilt, and guilt demands punishment.

For example, if I hold an unconscious belief that overeating is bad, I am unconsciously asking for punishment for it, and I will unconsciously punish myself by gaining weight.

Another example, if I believe that someone has hurt me and I see that wound as a sin, a judgment on that person, I unconsciously ask for revenge for the sin that I think has been committed. Therefore, I will suffer a punishment directed by the ego, which is the one who guides us when we believe in sin. I will suffer the punishment in the form of illness, physical pain, or any other symptom. The solution is not in remedying the symptom, but in giving us what the cause is, and the cause is always my unforgiven belief in sin. This symptom will be an opportunity to become aware and realize where it comes from.

We would be cured very quickly of any symptom if we recognized that none of these errors is a sin. It is simply a wrong perception, committed by the lack of faith that we have.

Can you inquire, what would Love do? How would Love respond to these errors? What would the voice of Love tell you?

Love forgives all errors, but for this, we have to keep in mind that they are not sins, but errors. The error of perception, I have perceived from the ego, and I want to see it from Love. The vision of Love is the true vision, and any other is just a perception, a mistake.

If your purpose is to heal the unconscious guilt, you use all the situations, people, scenarios, around you that generate conflict, to realize that you are using them to attack yourself. We must begin to recognize the "sins" we have made real, the events where we believe we are victims.

There is no healing until this is done, we have to reverse cause and effect. The symptom, or the effect I experience on my body and my environment is just that, an effect, and the true cause is in my mind, which is misperceiving.

The punishment applied for believing in scarcity is usually more scarcity, and so on. This is how the ego has us trapped in its circle of sin, guilt, and fear. And this circle ends when we deliver all these errors to our inner guide, to Love, for its reinterpretation.

Every feeling of discomfort, pain, dissatisfaction, however subtle, becomes conscious. I open myself to feel it, and I recognize that there is nothing external that is producing that, but that the cause is unconscious guilt. I make an act of surrender, to be able to see it in another way, and if you do this process truly, the miracle happens, the healing. I stop feeling that way, under the same circumstance. My liberation is greater every time, experiencing deep enjoyment every time—more time in my life.

You can do an exercise to identify where the areas of your unconscious beliefs reside in sin and guilt:

1.-Make a list of all the people or events that you see as a sin, a judgment, or something that deserves punishment. You can also use historical or social events, those that irritate you the most.

2.-Observe in your life story, who have you not completely forgiven? Where you refuse to look from the gaze of Love and feel resentment for that situation or person. Write everything that comes to mind.

3.-All these situations or people that you have not completely forgiven symbolize unconscious guilt. You see them as sins, and as long as you continue to have that perception, sin requires punishment.

Remember that all those "unforgiven" scenarios and people are not out there but inside our minds. As long as you don't change all the wrong perceptions, giving them to the voice of Understanding, and Love, so that you reinterpret it and see Love and innocence, they will demand and get you to punish yourself.

Play the Victim

People who suffer because life hits them require all the respect and space to elaborate on their suffering. Talking about a traumatic situation with another human being who listens compassionately causes the pain to shrink until, little by little, it becomes a permanent scar on the heart that allows life to continue. However, it is different from the one anticipated before the damage. Curiously, those people from whom authentic suffering springs tend to complain little —they even take refuge in silence—and try to rise under the cover of the enormous capacity for recovery of the human being. However, there are other types of individuals who use their misfortunes (real or imagined) to complain, feel sorry, or make you feel guilty. It is victimhood, a behavior that constitutes a real temptation for human beings because it has been repeated throughout the history of humanity (think of some rulers).

Look for Another Side

Coping is a concept used in psychology to refer to the set of strategies that a subject uses to deal with stressful events that occur in the environment or internal demands themselves. Some coping modalities are active and effective. Others are dysfunctional, and there is a risk of further damage.

Coping focused on changing reality can be harmful when the facts cannot be changed: we cannot always resolve a loss, some diseases, and even less death.

The Dramatic Triangle of Handling

For the psychologist Stephen Karpman, in human relationships we can fall—unconsciously sometimes and very deliberately others—into what he called 'The Dramatic Triangle.' This is a manipulation strategy in which (groups, institutions, and even, nations) these three roles are shared:

1. The victim: is not responsible for his misfortunes, seeking that others do for him what he should do for himself. To achieve his goal, he wants to be the center of attention and uses sentimentality, grief, and emotional blackmail. His traumatic event becomes his calling card.

2. The persecutor: he is always the victim of others whom he blames for his ill-fortune so that the image of himself is always safe, he has no problem and is right in everything he says and does. His tool is accusation and reproach until he makes you feel guilty (he is willing to look for your fault so as not to see his own) and afraid of a new accusation.

3. The savior: usually the well-meaning person who felt sorry for the victim's laments and overwhelmed if he does not do what the persecutor asks him to do. In return, he obtains self-assessment because by helping, he assumes that he is the best.

Victim

Marta has the role of savior in the family. Ana's husband has asked for a loan to pay his sister the 14,000 euros that he owes. It oscillated between feeling the need to do everything for Ana as she has always done and the anger of having to go into debt. The pressure from her mother and her friends (who do not pay the loan) has been decisive: "Poor thing, she is having a terrible time; she often fears her husband. How can you not help your sister?" They said. Society plays a key 'persecuting' role in the development of victimhood that favors abuse and compassion fatigue. Professor Danielle Giglioli, in his essay "Criticism of the victim," indicates that victimhood has been installed in our culture as a form of manipulation. We are not what we do but what we have suffered. "The victim is the new hero of our time," he says.

Presenting yourself as the affected, with sentimental tones included, is well seen (just turn on the television). In Ana's case, the first blow is inflicted on her by her husband. She provides the second with her ineffective response, the third by the culture of 'victimization' that needs 'poor little ones' to rescue to feel better by converting the world to a place where you can only be a victim or a villain. Marta (Ana's sister) is the collateral martyr who has to pay happily for helping and should not be regretted.

Tell Distorted or Half-Truths

In our day to day, we usually lie or tell half-truths in many of our conversations. Why do we do it? What are its consequences? And finally, what should we expect?

There is no worse coward than the one who makes constant use of half-truths. Because whoever combines truth with falsehood, sooner or later, evidences the complete lie. Tricks camouflaged with good manners are damaging and exhausting. Also, they tend to float, just like whole lies.

Unamuno said that there is no good fool. That

everyone, in their way, knows how to conspire and deploy effective tricks to catch us off guard. Now, if there is something that abounds in our society, it is not exactly the fools or the naive. The incomplete lie or the half-truth is the most familiar strategy that we see in almost all our contexts, especially in the spheres of politics.

The value of truth

Making use of headless truths or falsehoods with many short legs gives those who use them the feeling that they are doing nothing wrong. That he comes out unscathed from the responsibility, he has with the other. It seems that default pity discharges responsibilities. It's like someone saying, "I love you so much, but I need time." Or "I appreciate how you work, and we value all your effort, but we have to do without your contract for a few months."

The truth, although it hurts, is something that we all prefer and that we need at the same time. It is the only way we can move forward and join forces to deploy the appropriate psychological strategies with which to turn the page. We need to put aside the lack of certainty, and above all, that emotional instability that supposes not knowing. And finally, unmask the false illusions.

The bitter taste of half-truths

Oddly enough, the subject of lies and their psychological analysis is fairly recent. Freud barely touched on the subject. Until then, it was an aspect that remained in the hands of ethics and even theology and its relationship with morality. However, starting in the 1980s, social psychologists began to take an interest in and study the topic of deception in depth. Also, all the interesting phenomenology associated with it. All to confirm something that Nietzsche himself already said at the time: "lying is a condition of life."

We know that it can seem devastating because even though we are socialized from a very young age, in need to always tell the truth, little by little and from the age of 4, we realize that resorting to lies often involves getting certain benefits. Now, something that, in turn, becomes clear to us very early is that a direct falsehood and without real aroma is rarely profitable in the long term.

Research on lies or half-truths

On the other hand, as Professor Robert Feldman of the University of Massachusetts School of Psychology showed us, many of our most everyday conversations are riddled with those same incomplete truths. However, 98% of them are harmless, not harmful, and even functional (such as saying to a person with whom we do not have much confidence "that we are fine, pulling with this and that," when in fact, we are passing a complicated comment).

However, the remaining 2% do show that half-camouflaged truth, that perverse strategy where the half-truth fallacy executes an express deception by omission. There, also, the person tries to escape unscathed by justifying himself with the idea that since his lie is not complete, there is no offense.

CHAPTER 8

PSYCHOLOGICAL MANIPULATION TECHNIQUES

We are in the areas we most visit. It can be your supervisor, your neighbor upstairs, a coworker, a client, a near or distant relative, or some other. Think of people who know those methods of deception completely, and who use them to annoy us.

These people are not easy to spot even when they are among us. The features and traits of their personality are not clear. None wears an alarm bell on their forehead that they are a narcissist or a sociopath. So how do we get away from them?

How do I?

Those kinds of individuals feed on others' suffering. It's not, then, because you're poorer, more fragile, or different, but you're just another prey for them. Another total.

In certain cases, in which we are involved, we all have felt remorse or distrust. And the worst thing is that without learning, we sense it: not how, nor why. Yet the situation is that the consequences are splashing us out, weakening our confidence, complicating our lives, and our insecurities. Why do they do it without us knowing it?

Search for manipulators?

There are several forms of dishonest people in general: sociopaths, narcissists, liars, the so-called zombies in psychology. So, finding them is more a realistic matter than abstract. And you'll be quicker to predict if you've ever been a survivor of them.

However, it should be assumed that dishonest people's goals are very simple, persuasive and that they follow a certain template. Any of them include:

Nullify your will power: they seek to sow doubt and remain under your protection.

Destroy your self-esteem: get rid of everything you do or have done. They are not constructive, and they only try to focus on defects.

Passive-aggressive revenge: they punish you with their ignorance. When you need them, they leave you out; so, it is enough that you ask them something so that they give you a sit-down or they don't even speak to you again.

Misrepresent reality: They enjoy confusing people and creating discussions and misunderstandings of others. Having generated a dispute, they stay on the sidelines, having fun with other's disputes.

Learn How to Avoid Their Manipulation Techniques

The consequences of manipulation can generate a very deep mark on each of us. Therefore, it seems necessary that we know which manipulation techniques are used most frequently. The point is to learn to anticipate by ourselves and not to be their puppets.

These people often laugh at our opinions, hold us accountable, or make us feel guilty. They subtly attack, question us, delay what they are not interested in, feel sorry for, deny truths... Everything necessary to control the situation. But, what manipulation techniques do they use to achieve this?

- **Gaslighting**

Known as the "gaslight," it is one of the most insidious. "That has never happened," "You've imagined it," or "Are you crazy?" They are some of the words they use to manipulate and confuse your sense of truth, which would make you believe something has not happened.

Barton and Whitehead (1969) defined "gaslighting" as "the intentional pursuit of making a person appear insane and profiting from him." It instills in the victims an extreme sense of anguish and confusion, to such an extent that they stop trusting themselves, their memory, perception, or judgment.

In an investigation by Galán and Figeroa (2017), they describe making "gaslight" with denial of the damage caused, the elaboration of lies, offering false information, and disqualifying the feelings towards the victim. It is also a method to confuse the partner, manipulate, blame, and downplay the experiences, and thus destroy the victim through his mental health.

The attacker's communication to the victim is hostile through silences, complaints, damaging jokes and humiliations, threats, etc. The consequences on the victim, according to the authors, can be several:

- **Guilty feeling**
- **Disorientation**
- **Panic**
- **Anger**
- **Duel**
- **Low self-esteem**

- **Lack of autonomy**
- **Emotional dependence**
- **Alcohol consumption**
- **Even suicide**
- **Projection**

The manipulator passes his negative traits to someone else, or shifts blame for his behaviors. The narcissists and psychopaths use this, claiming that the evil that surrounds them is not their fault, but yours.

- **Nonsense conversations**

Ten minutes of conversation. That is the time that you surely take to leave the talk. The manipulators say nonsense, illogical explanations, smoke screens, past events ...

They just mess around. They make monologues and try to wrap you up with their repetition. Advice? Cut early. And if you can leave after 5 minutes, the better. Your mind will thank you.

- **Generalizations and disqualifications**

They make ambiguous, general comments. They can seem intelligent, but they are lazy. Their conclusions are too general; their goal is to dismiss you and destroy your opinions.

For example, "You always want to be right," "Everything bothers you," "You never agree." Keep calm. You can pull irony, with a simple "Thank you," or by ignoring him with a resounding, "I think you're a little upset, we'll talk later."

- **The absurd**

Remember that they seek to undermine your morale and make you rethink what you believe in. They may put things in your mouth you didn't know, they'll make you believe they have the superpower to "read your mind." But no, they're all tricks. Simulated claudication will support you. You tell him he's right to believe that, but you're always holding on to your stance. You can also respond with a "voucher" or with laconic phrases to their blackmail.

The main thing is that you take away from their hands your self-esteem. They think that is what they want to throw on the ground to control you. Once they have weakened you, the task for them is much easier.

No greater contempt does not appreciate it.

- **Kindness Costume**

"Yes, but ...". If you just bought a house, they will tell you what a shame it is you still don't have one on the beach; If you have become more elegant than ever, they will point out that other earrings would have been better for you ... If you have completed an impeccable report, they will notice that the staple is not properly fixed.

But that should not affect you, and you should know what you are worth! Your achievements and your virtues are worth more than their manipulation techniques. Don't give them credibility. Hang out with people who spend more time stressing what's right and cheering you on; the ones that flatter you when they have to and issue constructive, not destructive criticism.

Resist his attack of rage

When you oppose a manipulator, it is normal for his anger to increase within a few seconds, especially if you don't play along: his tolerance for frustration is usually not very high. It is possible that he begins to speak outrageously and even insults you and refers to you in derogatory and pejorative terms. It is the result of their mistrust.

These are the most subtle and frequent manipulation techniques these people use to humiliate you. Master your emotions and keep a cool head: the only way to escape control. If you don't succumb, they'll get tired and end up looking for another victim. Life away from toxic people is much better.

CHAPTER 9

THE ROLE OF DEFENCE

Assertiveness is a characteristic of our way of being that allows us to express our emotions freely and without altering ourselves. It allows us to defend our rights, tastes, and interests, directly, simply, and appropriately, without assaulting others and without consenting to being attacked.

Being assertive means that you have a healthy relationship with yourself (self-esteem) and with the people around you. That is, an assertive person has a natural balance that allows him to socialize in a fluid and healthy way, without leaning towards passivity or aggressiveness, thinking, acting and communicating appropriately and adaptively.

The most assertive people feel more sure of themselves. That is why healthy self-esteem plays an important role to have appropriate behaviors in interpersonal communication; without making a value judgment or showing passivity or aggressiveness towards the other person.

All people, no matter their personality traits, can use Assertiveness to improve their relationships with the people around them and themselves because Assertiveness is a skill that can be learned and modified.

Where can we locate the form of assertive interpersonal behavior?

Assertive communication is somewhere in the middle of 3 other forms of communication:

Aggressive communication: This style of communication occurs when we are not able to respect the ideas or actions of others. There is no empathy or we do not take into account the feelings of the other.

Passive communication: it is a style in which the person does not defend his interests, allows third parties to decide for him, or does not comment on his true feelings and does not express a disagreement. People with passive communication are little conflictive, but it has the disadvantage that they can feel frustrated or resentful at some point.

Passive-aggressive communication: A person who communicates passive-aggressively does not put himself or the other in the foreground but communicates poorly or in a confused manner. He often uses excuses and has little personal ambition.

Assertive style: When communication is assertive, it means that our interests or points of view are just as important as someone else's. One learns from the other person, and both people end up satisfied. It is the ideal communication and behavior, relationships benefit, and the interlocutors respect themselves and those around them.

Examples of assertiveness

A child is playing alone; another child approaches, and they end up playing together, sharing their toys without any alteration, enjoying the moment.

A person comes up smoking and asks if the smell of tobacco bothers us. By telling him we don't like tobacco, he understands it and walks away.

Assertive Communication Techniques or how to work on assertiveness

One of the first attempts by behavioral clinicians to improve patients' social skills is focused on an extensive set of procedures and skills, generally called assertive training. Assertiveness training was a method to help people overcome anxiety aroused by interpersonal encounters.

The explanation of assertive training was presented as follows:

- When anxiety inhibits the behaviors required in interpersonal relationships, the person is almost inevitably at a disadvantage when he is face to face with other people... His unexpressed impulse continues to reverberate within him and that can cause somatic symptoms, including pathological changes and a wide variety of clinical problems, such as social anxiety.

- It has been used in the treatment of diseases such as social dysfunction, alcoholism and depression. ... In the first clinical work on assertive training, the expression of irritation, resentment and feelings of anger was emphasized in a socially appropriate way. Anxiety would gradually be inhibited since it was assumed to be incompatible with the assertive expression of feelings. In assertive training, operational aspects were also considered, that is, acts of assertive interpersonal capacity were programmed that agreed with favorable consequences in the person's natural social environment, thus being reinforced.

- More recently, however, assertive training has expanded to include the expression of positive feelings, such as the ability to convey praise, affection, and approval.

Some skills to train assertiveness:

It is important to identify what you feel through self-observation. Do you feel anxiety, tension, sweat? In this case it is important to learn self-control techniques that help us relax, such as muscle relaxation, mindfulness, etc.

- Social skills techniques
- Understand what thinking errors are
- Understand the different levels of communication and learn communication skills
- Know what the defense mechanisms are
- Learn cognitive flexibility and work possible blocks
- Assertive response techniques
- Having adequate non-verbal communication
- Impulse control

Why is being assertive so important

Some people with interpersonal behavior deficits never seem to have learned appropriate social skills. Because of these deficits, the person has great difficulty in obtaining the types of social reinforcement required. In the absence of an appropriate social interpretation, different forms of deviant behavior are reinforced, including illusory language, periods of crying, and antisocial behavior, which is maintained by the attention that they invariably arouse from others.

Causes of assertiveness deficit and the importance of self-esteem

Several researchers argue that assertiveness has a direct relationship with self-esteem.

Self-esteem is the feeling of appreciation or rejection that accompanies the global assessment that we make of ourselves. This self-assessment is based on our perception of specific qualities, such as the ability to relate to others, physical appearance, character traits, etc.

People who do not consider themselves valuable usually choose not to actively defend their rights, creating a vicious circle by undermining their self-esteem again when their rights are not respected.

Other reasons for the assertiveness deficit would be the influence of certain social and labor stereotypes. In some highly hierarchical cultures or organizations, submission is established as the accepted behavior in certain roles and genres.

The emotional state also influences the response that can be given at a specific moment. A high-stress load can cause excessively aggressive or passive behavior, sometimes generating greater anxiety due to the rejection that the response itself causes in others.

It was also discovered that assertiveness has to do with the degree of maturity of each individual. As well as the emotional and intrinsic factors of personality, people whose self-esteem is high tend to develop a higher degree of assertiveness. The differences between assertive people and those who do not develop this ability lie in the lack of character, as well as ideologies, lack of confidence in their abilities or, that they lack clear objectives when communicating.

Assertive behavior can be trained and, in this way, increase the number of situations in which we will have an assertive response.

What is an assertive response?

The assertive response is a tool that makes it easier to carry on smarter conversations without bullying, offending, or humiliating anyone, creating empathy with the speaker. Your knowledge can be very useful for conflict resolution.

Being assertive in a conversation allows us to verbally engage intelligently without verbal aggressiveness when defending a position on something. The assertive response makes it easy to find the balance between aggressiveness and passivity in an argument.

The term "assertive behavior" is used broadly to cover all socially acceptable expressions in an appropriate way of personal rights and feelings.

Dialogue with assertive responses or assertive communication

What are the main assertive response techniques to successfully tackle an argument?

The way to have a conversation or discussion with another person depends on our personality and the purpose of the conversation. When we have discrepancies in opinions during a conversation, it can cause psychological and physical discomfort. By being skillful in using assertiveness responses, we are more agile in expressing our thoughts, desires, and feelings, we maintain our well-being and even strengthen our self-esteem.

Here are some of the resources to respond assertively that may be helpful in a discussion or under pressure from others:

Fogbank. Agree on the possibility of what the other says. It is effective when they criticize us. The "fog bank" is useful to avoid entering into a discussion about who has the last word or not. We let the words enter this cloud as if we haven't heard anything.

Example: - You have gained a lot of weight. - Maybe I have to start taking care of myself.

Negative assertion. Clearly say something in me that I do not like or that something is bad according to the opinions or attack of the interlocutor. We react to fair criticism without too many excuses or justifications.

Example: - You are late. - It's true, sorry.

Self-disclosure. Assertively disclose personal information.

Example: - But how can you eat that? - Because I like it.

Broken record. Repeat the request persistently and calmly. It is very useful when we meet a very persistent person. In this case, it works to repeat the request over and over again in a calm way, as if it were a mantra, to reach our goal.

Example: - We can go out tonight - I don't feel like it - It makes for a nice night - I don't feel like it - etc.

Assertive agreement. Admit that I have made a mistake but separating it from being a good or bad person. It is useful in situations where the person is right to be angry, but we do not agree with the way to tell us.

Example: - I've been waiting for you. - Yes, I forgot about the date we had to eat. I am usually more responsible.

Assertive question. Directly ask the details that have led to criticism or attack on me. We do not question what they have told us, and we use the "assertive question" to understand the attack without denying, defending ourselves, counterattacking, justifying, etc. The assertive question helps us understand why they are criticizing.

Example: - I understand that you do not like the way I acted the other night in the meeting. What bothered you? What is it in my way of speaking that you dislike?

Deviation. Shift the discussion towards the analysis of what happens between my interlocutor and me, leaving aside the topic of it.

Example: - We are moving past the question, and we will end up talking about past things.

Simulated claudication. Giving ground, giving part of the reason to the interlocutor, but without actually giving it up. You have to agree with the other person's argument but without agreeing to change your position.

Example: - You may be right, surely it could be more generous. Maybe I shouldn't be so tough, but ...

Ignore. This technique is recommended when the interlocutor is wrong, and you can be nervous, upset, angry, etc. In this situation, it is better to ignore the reason why the interlocutor seems to be angry and to postpone the discussion until he has calmed down. Empathy is recommended at this time.

Example: - I see that you are very angry, so we better talk about it at another time.

Breakdown of the process. Respond to criticism or provocations with a single word or brief phrases.

Example: - Yes ... No... Maybe...

Assertive irony. It is about responding ironically or positively to hostile provocation or criticism.

Example: - You are boastful.... - Okay, thanks.

Assertive postponement. When we find ourselves upset or angry, it is simply a matter of postponing the response to the "attack" until we feel calm and able to respond to it appropriately.

<u>Example:</u> - Yes, it is a very interesting topic, but we will discuss it later. I do not want to talk about that right now. (Because I'm wrong)

Thanks to being skillful in using assertive responses, we can express ourselves freely and clearly, respecting ourselves and respecting the rights of our interlocutors.

The assertive response can be a very valuable tool for:

- company managers,
- public persons,
- teachers,
- family relationships, etc.

Being assertive is essential to our quality of life; Through the ability of assertive communication, we can successfully manage interpersonal relationships, achieve tranquility and personal satisfaction, and create a good environment.

CHAPTER 10

THE POWER OF EMOTIONAL INTELLIGENCE

Most researchers in psychology consider emotional intelligence as the most important ability to succeed in life. Studies have shown that, for example, activities related to high IQ are only useful in 20% of everyday situations. On the other hand, emotional intelligence is a type of broader capacity that includes both internal and social understanding, making it essential for such fundamental factors as choosing the right partner or the ideal job.

Here we review the main elements that have been found important in the process to acquire and develop emotional intelligence. This quality is not innate, but can be developed, and helps us for a large number of routine questions, from knowing how to solve problems, until we understand each other.

What Is Emotional Intelligence?

Emotional Intelligence per se is a concept that is quite recent in the study of human behavior; It was only in the 20th century, mainly in the second half, that efforts began to try to define its nature, trying to make a different classification to cognitive intelligence.

It was from 1995 that the work called Emotional Intelligence by Daniel Goleman managed to spread the term, from a compilation of scientific research that allowed to organize and begin to define its characteristics better.

In general, Emotional Intelligence is considered as the set of behaviors and forms of knowledge that allow us to assimilate and respond in a useful way. Both towards our own emotions, as well as about impulses from the outside, which allows us to develop the better way in a social environment, and thus achieve a more efficient way of achieving objectives that allow the individual to feel happy and satisfied.

Although Emotional Intelligence has a large component of subjectivity and is difficult to measure, various scientific experiments have been developed to understand better and define its essence, based not only on human behavior but also on the neurological processes that are carried out.

Various theorists also agree that emotional intelligence does not lead to responses that have to be good or bad, but rather that they can generate positive or negative consequences. For example, a traffic light in a person who does not properly use emotional intelligence can result in an accident, which is notoriously a response with mostly negative results, compared to that person who acted in moderation, and avoids a further incident. Big and meaningless.

Emotional Intelligence is another type of intelligence

Through multiple scientific and social experiments, it has been possible to differentiate emotional intelligence from other types of intelligence, particularly linked to cognitive abilities. The most widely accepted definition in this field is that of Howard Gardner, who lists intelligence such as musical, spatial-visual, mathematical logic, linguistic verbal, and kinesthetic body, which refer more to intelligence that denotes a certain type of physical ability.

In this same widely accepted definition of intelligence, other types are also included, such as interpersonal and intrapersonal intelligence. These are more related to the psychological skills of both internal and external understanding, respectively.

It is these two classifications also that Goleman takes up and mentions as the main types of

Emotional Intelligence, and which refer to the ability to regulate human relationships, as well as understanding, valuation, and internal development.

Main Elements of Emotional Intelligence

In the analysis of Emotional Intelligence, not only does the internal and external focus influence, as we have mentioned, but these are also combined with two essential behaviors: interpretation, which is how we assimilate the perceptions and knowledge acquired, and the response, which is the result of the analysis performed. In the conjunction of each of these perspectives, four main elements are generated, which we analyze below.

- **Emotional self-awareness**

This is the ability to understand not only what we are feeling, but also the reasons for having those emotions or feelings. It is essentially about the ability to understand yourself, value yourself, appreciate yourself, which also involves the series of acquired values and paradigms.

This element is particularly essential for such basic and important questions as knowing how to express our feelings to other people because this is where the motivations and beliefs that govern our way of thinking can be clearly understood.

- **Emotional self-control**

This approach essentially refers to the ability to regulate our emotions, that is, the internal emotional response. This type of emotional intelligence is important, for example, to contain and assimilate feelings of sadness, frustration, or anger, to name a few examples.

It should be noted that through scientific research such as that of Joseph LeDoux—also mentioned in Goleman's masterpiece—it was possible to identify an important neurological factor in this process of self-control. It normally works as follows: the Emotional reasoning process usually begins in the thalamus, which is where the impulses from sensory organs such as the eyes or ears come from. Then they are passed to the neocortex, which is the area of the brain where these data are recorded and analyzed. Next they are sent to the lobes prefrontal where the stimuli are organized and try to be understood, making a detailed analysis of the context, background and situation, to then send the final signal to the limbic system. This is the one that will generate the consequent response; however, it is not in all cases that thoughts flow with this same efficiency.

LeDoux discovered that, especially in situations where impulsive and fast acting was performed, the neurological pathway took a kind of shortcut. And instead of sending impulses from the thalamus to the neocortex, it diverted them to the amygdala, where a response occurred. Almost instinctively from the most vivid memories of the moment and sending it directly to the limbic system; that is, without going through the prefrontal lobes or the neocortex, and thus avoiding the main analysis processes to resolve a situation.

The researchers point out that this reaction is understandable, particularly from a human evolutionary condition originating from ancient times, where it was important to have a capacity to respond quickly to possible and constant threats. This being, in reality, a natural protection system. However, specialists consider that this type of reaction could be somewhat discordant in our times since a greater proportion of reasoned and non-impulsive responses is required.

This is where their emotional intelligence can work, especially people with neurosis problems or who rely too much on spontaneous impulses. Because from deeper reasoning and based on broader judgment, they can make more accurate decisions.

- **Empathy**

Empathy is essentially the ability to understand other people's vision and thoughts; sometimes it is confused with listening and paying attention to others, although it is not just about this. But the ability to see things from a third-party perspective, which can allow us to understand other people's perspectives better, and in this way to be able to develop a more efficient social exercise.

This ability represents what the individual feels about others, which is also usually a type of emotional intelligence important to have a greater tolerance and understanding towards the outside. In the same way, it can help us to resolve a wide variety of conflicts. For example, family fights, since in this way you can adopt a broader understanding of things, allowing solutions to be found, also considering other people's needs; after all, man does not stop being a social being, which is why this becomes an important factor for better social development.

- **Social skills**

And if empathy represents the conception of others, social skills become the answer, the consequence, or in other words, our reaction to the exterior in the face of these internally defined paradigms and judgments.

This element of emotional intelligence allows us to develop adequately, also according to the main conventions and norms of healthy coexistence, and of course, also according to the context of the individual. Here the social capacity is shown if you have developed emotional intelligence, or in contrast, you can also adopt sociopathic behaviors.

And while the primary focus of emotional intelligence is based on these four newly exposed elements, some also add to adaptability and self-motivation as two other important factors within intrapersonal intelligence.

Habits of People with High Emotional Intelligence

After multiple studies with high academic rigor, it has also been possible to identify certain characteristic behaviors that are usually present in people with a developed emotional intelligence:

- **Extroverts**

One of the characteristics that distinguish people with developed emotional intelligence is their ability to express their emotions and ways of thinking with great ease; that is, they are quite extroverted.

This ability becomes even more marked in women since an energetic character can be developed, where the woman is not afraid to make spontaneous reactions with great security either.

- **Sociable**

The outward qualities of a person with high emotional intelligence are also important abilities to cope with great ease in a social environment. Generally speaking, they do not find it difficult to strike up conversations with strangers, and they have a great capacity to adapt to different environments and situations.

- **With trust**

Another characteristic quality is trust, which has two main meanings; since on the one hand, they have a greater capacity to be able to trust people— of course, those who, in their opinion, meet the requirements of a trustworthy person.

And on the other hand, this idea also refers to self-confidence; since emotional intelligence not only allows us to interpret our characteristics, conditions, and qualities. But also to assimilate them, value them, and of course, take advantage of them with a higher level of security.

- **Ethical vision**

It has also been shown that people with this type of intelligence tend to have a higher level of social commitment, since they seek to put into practice the moral and established values, as much as possible in aspects of daily life.

In the case of men, for example, it is usually exemplified in practice through the determination in environmentalist, political, humanitarian positions. Or those that in the person's opinion are appropriate and are also part of the common good of that which we are also part of.

- **Leadership**

Some of the important skills of people who develop their emotional intelligence are those related to the ability to convince, and of course, also to manipulate other people.

These types of behaviors are characteristic qualities of people with a broad sense of leadership, which of course, has a strong basis in the trust they have acquired, but in this case, it is precisely the response expressed in behaviors with outstanding abilities and leadership.

- **Kind and loving**

Another outstanding skill mentioned in the different bibliographies on emotional intelligence is the ability to express feelings more fluidly and directly. This is reflected through behaviors such as affection and love.

People who develop this ability also tend to have a stable emotional life. They are not only able to find a better partner, more related to the expectations and desires of the individual, but as a consequence they are also more consistent and respectful of relationships. This allows you to have greater stability in this regard.

This is particularly noticeable in the female sex, and is also related to the ability to have a full sex life; unlike those who only develop their IQ, and those who usually have greater problems such as anxiety or difficulty in fully enjoying their sex life.

- **Joyful people**

And as a consequence of all these abilities, people with advanced emotional intelligence also tend to have a higher degree of satisfaction in general. Which is why they tend to maintain an appearance not only outgoing but also cheerful, sometimes joking and generally with a much more positive outlook.

The importance of emotional intelligence as a factor to regulate, assimilate and dilute negative issues is an important capability. It allows us to maintain a positive posture towards life, which is why visibly happier people are generally generated. This also means a noticeable behavioral difference compared to those who only develop their IQ and those who tend to maintain a colder, more balanced, and less expressive posture.

Emotional Intelligence in working life

One of the important points where emotional intelligence can be put into practice is in terms of working life. Of course, starting with the choice of our profession or trade, for which an exhaustive analysis of both skills and expectations must be carried out.

This type of intelligence is also essential to develop within a job, particularly in cases where teamwork is required. The ability to adapt, as well as leadership skills, can be factors of success for the individual with this type of intelligence developed.

This is important to measure since according to reference works on the subject, it has been documented that the development of the IQ, interferes only in a fifth of the factors that determine the success of a person. This explains why individuals who are obsessed with having a perfect grade during their academic development, neglect essential factors of emotional intelligence, which often ends up obstructing the professional development of the individual.

And although to achieve success, there are also factors such as social status, and even luck, it is currently considered that emotional intelligence also plays a crucial factor. It is involved with a greater variety of essential success factors, particularly in comparison to cognitive intelligence.

Emotional Intelligence can be developed

The most reputable researchers on the subject also agree that emotional intelligence is not only innate, but also has a great capacity to be learned and developed. This is part of the process that is normally known as maturation, and which essentially means the human capacity to be able to make decisions based on a broader criterion and analysis. In contrast, as many factors as possible are taken into consideration, thus seeking to reach more successful solutions.

This type of intelligence is developed mainly and

with greater emphasis from own experiences; hence famous sayings such as "no one is cheating on someone else's head," for example, although in reality, the human being also can learn from external or third-party experiences. Still, you have to have a high level of empathy to be able to assimilate this kind of knowledge. To incorporate it within the framework of judgments that are part of the neural process in the neocortex, that is, in the chain formed by values and paradigms.

What is an Emotional Intelligence test?

This type of test seeks to measure in some way the level of development of this type of intelligence, although mainly based on certain specific elements. In this case, unlike IQ, there is no fully agreed scientific procedure here to design an exact evaluation of this type. Mainly because more subjective factors are involved and, therefore, they are more difficult to measure or assess, since you never have such clear answers.

In IQ tests, for example, there is full scientific certainty of obtaining the volume of a three-dimensional geometric body according to the number and size of its edges; but on the other hand, in emotional intelligence, it is not possible to determine with the same precision which is the correct or incorrect answer. Much has to do with the interpretation and even the same concept and value framework of each person or region.

In this sense, the tests of emotional intelligence are rather informal experiments to know certain tendencies about specific situations or elements; without having, to date, a formula to give a precise qualification to the development of this type of intelligence.

Busting the Myths About Emotional Intelligence

MYTH 1. The most emotionally intelligent people tend to be more likable and outgoing.

It is very typical that when we create in our minds the image of an emotionally intelligent person, we think of someone very kind, popular and with many friends. Or if we know someone like that, we label them as emotionally intelligent. However, introversion-extroversion is a different dimension of the person, which has nothing to do with emotional intelligence.

A person can be very introverted and have a high degree of EI, and a very extroverted can have very low EQ. The first, the introvert, may have high knowledge of her emotional world and know how to manage it for the benefit of the goals she wants to achieve in life (e.g., managing her anxiety before an exam or in a discussion where you have to be assertive). The second, the extrovert, may not have that knowledge and ability (e.g., being blocked before the exam or not daring to attend, or speaking and speaking a lot in a discussion but not acting assertively, instead of saying things clearly and in a respectful manner).

MYTH 2. People with a high degree of Emotional Intelligence are very emotional people.

It is common to misinterpret emotional intelligence in which it is understood as the ability to express, not save, emotions. For this reason, those who are very emotionally expressive, who "do not keep their emotions," are labeled with a higher EQ. This is another clear myth about emotional intelligence.

Although the recognition and expression of one's emotions are indeed part of EI, taking only this part as the key element can lead us to misunderstandings. Emotional intelligence has to do with a series of abilities such as "accurately perceiving, valuing and expressing emotions; the ability to access and generate feelings that facilitate punishment; the ability to understand emotions and emotional intelligence, and the ability to control emotions that foster emotional and mental development" (Mayer and Salovey).

According to Mayer and Salovey (parents of EI), emotional intelligence would consist of four major skills related to emotions: 1- perception-expression, 2- thought facilitation, 3- understanding and analysis, and 4- reflexive regulation. Therefore, a very emotionally expressive person may have the first skill (and sometimes not even that) but may not have the other three. For example, when faced with the challenge of starting a new job, you can be very conscious and expressive about how you feel (perhaps fear, insecurity, anxiety ...). But not knowing how to use your emotions to facilitate positive thoughts (skill 2). Nor to understand more deeply that fear and insecurity and its relation with what one thinks and says, nor the reason why these sudden changes of emotions come to one, from fear to joy, followed by insecurity and anguish, etc. (skill 3). Nor being able to regulate those emotions that block you by taking perspective and not letting them block or condition you too much in your first interactions at work (skill 4).

MYTH 3. Women, in general, have more emotional intelligence than men.

The third of the myths about emotional intelligence is also widespread. This belief is very common. Part of one of the most widespread gender stereotypes: women are more emotional and men more rational. According to Natalio Extremera, one of the great experts in EI, "the scientific evidence on the subject is controversial and, globally, gender differences in emotional intelligence are small and depend on many factors such as age, educational level, specific training or culture. "

The important thing, from Extremera's perspective (which follows the line of work of Salovey and Mayer), is that each person knows their emotional intelligence profile. They know their strengths and weaknesses in each of the four dimensions of EI, and seek to improve progressively.

Therefore, it is not a question of having more or less EI than someone else, which, although it is measured with some tests, is still difficult to calibrate and compare. I'm going to give an example of two people. One could be defined— never exempt from subjectivity—as having less EI than the other. But whom is very aware of his strengths and weaknesses and has a clear improvement attitude. And on the other hand, the

144

other that, having much more emotional skills—and scoring better on tests—is not aware of his improvement points (he has blind spots that he does not recognize). Possibly, although on paper—the tests—the first would have a lower level of EI. We could almost qualify it as more EI due to the growth potential he reflects and because self-knowledge itself is closely related to present EI and future potential.

CHAPTER 11

WHY DO YOU NEED EMOTIONAL INTELLIGENCE IN YOUR BUSINESS?

If you are a manager, director or boss, you should read this chapter about emotional intelligence. It will help you improve your leadership.

In a world of business which promotes and admires a hypercompetitive culture and in which the achievement of objectives seems an end that justifies all means, talk about emotional intelligence seems somewhat misplaced.

However, for Leonardo N'Haux, president of Qualtop Group, a company that seeks to maximize organizational capabilities through processes of innovation and agility, these skills are absolutely necessary to travel through the corporate corridors, the World Economic Forum reports.

For his part, the psychologist and writer Daniel Goleman, affirms emotional intelligence is the ability to motivate ourselves. The ability to persevere despite frustrations, to control impulses, to regulate our own moods, and to empathize and trust in the others.

Here are three corporate examples where emotional intelligence can help you:

1. Negotiation

In any negotiation situation you have, your emotional skills serve you to connect better with your interlocutor. In a negotiation, what you are looking for is a result that the two of you will be happy with. That is the best result that you can have from a negotiation and, in that sense, emotional skills can help you a lot.

2. Construction of work teams

In the construction of work teams you have to look for needs that are complementary and achieve a synergy such that everyone feels they are going for the same goal and commit themselves. In this sense, being able to communicate this and reach people's emotions, that is, emotionally convince them that it is worth the effort, the challenge, is key to that.

3. Conflict resolution

You have to understand that people, in general, do not fight for pleasure. In general, there is an emotional clash between needs, and between different positions. Such that, when you analyze it from the emotional components of the problem and manage to transmit it to the people who are intervening in the conflict, you help a lot of things to be unleashed in a much more agile way and for the benefit of all.

Why Is Emotional Intelligence Important in The Workplace?

The inability to understand and deal with human emotions is an unfortunate trend in western society. This trend has spread to many areas of life, especially the workplace. Emotions often stay on the doorstep when you start working and this has devastating effects not only for companies, but also on employees (from assistant to CEO). Because we are emotional people.

Every day we make emotionally charged decisions. We believe Plan A is better than Plan B, and sometimes we make decisions based on our visceral emotions or feelings. As much as we try to base decision making on rational methods, emotions influence. Understanding the origin and source of these emotions will help us make better decisions. Also, when we work as a team, we will be more in tune with each other.

With globalization, emotional intelligence is more important than ever. In an environment where teams are intercultural, multi-generational and global, the complexity of the interactions of emotions and the way they are expressed increases.

Emotional intelligence in the workplace comes down to understanding, expressing and managing good relationships, and problem solving under pressure.

Applications of emotional intelligence in the company

Since the initial research was published in 1990, innovative organizations have begun testing how to integrate Emotional Intelligence into training and hiring for a competitive advantage. It is becoming increasingly clear that these skills are the foundation of high-performance organizations.

Multiple emotional intelligence implementation strategies have been used in the company, particularly in leadership and culture development, and for selection and retention. Emotional intelligence skills are measurable and can be learned and improved through training. The most effective implementation strategies seek to integrate emotional intelligence into the organizational culture.

Benefits of applying emotional intelligence to the organization

Benefits and good results have been demonstrated in many areas of the organization:

- Increased sales performance through recruiting and training emotionally smarter salespeople.
- Better customer service by hiring customer service agents with higher emotional intelligence ratings.
- Superior leadership performance, developing and recruiting executives with high Emotional Intelligence.
- Better team performance, with higher productivity and profit growth.
- Using emotional intelligence in training and organizational change initiatives reduces costs associated with turnover, absenteeism, and poor performance.

Results of applying emotional intelligence in business

Research has provided clear data that emotionally intelligent leaders are more successful. Studies in large companies show these results:

- At PepsiCo, executives selected for

emotional intelligence skills generated 10% more productivity.

- Sellers with a high emotional intelligence index at L'Oreal brought in $2.5 million more in sales.
- An emotional intelligence initiative at Sheraton helped increase market share by 24%.

Emotionally Intelligent People Handle Pressure Better

Pressure has to do with Stress, with what is happening, and with the demand that we have. But beyond that, stress is the inability that people show to deal effectively with a stressor. This means that stress does not affect all people in the same way, it depends a lot on our ability to handle situations. Therefore, emotional intelligence has become the key competence if we are to understand why some people are successful, and others are not in an increasingly competitive environment.

There are two key elements that we must consider if we are talking about high organizational performance.

The first element is self-management—the ability we have to manage ourselves. Self-knowledge—the ability to know how we are and how stressors are affecting us. When a person knows how to recognize their emotions and knows what is happening inside them, they have a greater ability to direct what is happening to them adequately. So, we take a break and realize when we are going out of our boxes, see how it affects us and become aware of how situations can overtake us. Then we know how to act, how to go out and take a break knowing that is not the best time to resolve the issue. That is to be aware of yourself.

Self-management is the ability we have to channel our emotional energy to more productive levels. To levels that take us to better control of what is happening to us. How do we channel those emotions? Through thoughts, the way we are interpreting them, and the situations that happen to us. So the drama that happens to us as human beings is not because of the situations that happen outside, but rather because of the way we interpret them in our mental universe. Channeling the correct thoughts can adequately direct the emotions to be able to motivate them. That element of self-motivation, so linked to self-regulation, is capable of transforming and changing the emotional level that we have at that moment. So instead of diving into depression, thinking about all the debts, why not direct your thoughts to more creative places and say things such as: "This situation is a challenge that I have to meet, what I can do right now to get ahead of this situation." Channeling energy correctly is what is going to make you resolve the situation or not, but this is a skill that you have to develop. Generate discipline so that you do not fall prey to your emotions, but that thoughts are capable of guiding your emotions.

The other component is the ability to manage the relationships we have with others; work, home, friends, etc. This is essential. We have to learn to recognize the emotions of others. You achieve this through a great tool called empathy. What we have heard many times is that we must put ourselves in the shoes of others, but also put them on and walk about 5 km with them to understand what it feels like. This means realizing what is happening in the mental universe of people, how emotions are affecting them, what worries them, or what motivates them. If I can detect those mechanisms that trigger your emotions and I have the knowledge to be able to properly direct your emotions in search of the results that we are all looking for, that is called influence.

After managing emotions comes another important point—social skills. This refers to how I manage relationships with other people so that I can generate results, synergy, and collaboration to direct ourselves towards a common goal. The social skills that are very important to develop include effective communication, assertiveness, and negotiation. These are the skills that allow me to work in a team to achieve results. I'm only going to do that with the right language, the right arguments, the right whys so that people can join the common goal.

If you are a leader who has a vision, but you do not know how to share or transmit it to the emotional world of people, no matter how capable or intelligent you are, or how much experience you have, you will not be able to go very far. Yes, your technical skills are very important, no one denies that knowledge will be decisive for success, but unfortunately, it is not the most important thing. The ability you have to manage your emotions and manage the emotions of others, to manage to direct your efforts towards a shared objective, that is what generates great results. Daniel Goleman, in 1995, said it clearly: "Emotional competence is twice as important as technical competence when it comes to explaining top management performance."

Emotionally Intelligent People Are Better Decision-Makers

"Colder, more rational people make better decisions."

"I was wrong because I got carried away by my emotions."

"Psychopaths are evolved beings because their emotions do not influence them."

Such statements are topics that I keep listening to and reading, and they are not true. We cannot criminalize our emotional side, which makes us human, intuitive, sensitive, and creative when it comes to solving our conflicts.

Emotions influence us every day, and it is inevitable. Therefore, it is essential to enhance our emotional intelligence, because, in this way, we will be able to recognize both our feelings and those of others to value successful decisions, avoiding impulsiveness and risk. Emotions are signs of our inner world, we cannot ignore them, but yes, through self-awareness, 'select' constructive emotions and discard those that block us. The challenge is learning to use emotions effectively.

Science supports it; a 2013 study by the University of Toronto concluded that we are prey to emotional influence all the time and that emotionally intelligent people don't remove all emotions from their decision-making, They just ignore the emotions that have nothing to do with the decision and take into account those that are relevant.

"People often decide influenced by emotions that have nothing to do with the decisions they are making," explained Stéphane Côté, co-author of the study. Therefore, those with higher levels of emotional intelligence can make better decisions. However, those who have less emotional intelligence but become aware of what they are feeling and manage to separate it from the choice they must make can also block the emotions of others that influence their decisions.

Côté suggests that if the person feels anxiety or other emotion before making a decision, pause instead of taking it immediately. "You have to pay attention only to the feelings that are relevant to the decisions that are made, " the researchers stressed. Also, they clarify that we must not only pay attention to the negative emotions that a person may experience but also to the positive ones, which can also condition us erroneously.

Five Ways Emotional Intelligence Helps You Make Decisions

According to the psychiatry faculty of the National Autonomous University of Mexico (UNAM), emotional intelligence is "the ability to perceive your feelings and those of others, distinguish between them and use that information to guide thought and conduct of oneself." Learn to manage your emotions:

1. **Identify.** Emotions are signs that show our inner and social world to those around us. Knowing how to identify them helps us maintain a better ability to communicate with others.
2. **Use.** The proper use of emotions helps us guide our thoughts to solve the problems that arise.
3. **Understand.** Each of our emotions has different causes that, if we learn to detect, we can understand why we react in a certain way at a specific time.
4. **Drive.** It intelligently incorporates emotions in the way of solving problems, which helps us know how to manage our behavior.
5. **Control.** Emotional intelligence goes beyond the ability to control a bad mood. It plays a very important role in the quality of

life since by putting the above points into practice, people can learn to use emotions effectively.

According to research carried out by the Dr. Rafael Belloso Chacín University (URBE), in Venezuela, 83% of the people evaluated who put this technique into practice, learned to regulate their emotions. This benefited their self-knowledge and control of them.

The use of emotional intelligence helps to create awareness about our actions by contemplating the importance of our emotions and the impact they generate on our behavior and way of life.

People with High EQ Handle Conflicts Better

It is important to know how to handle conflict because they have become part and parcel of our everyday lives. In this section, I will attempt to demystify how this can be carried out properly.

It is possible to achieve peace of mind. I cannot promise you that it will be easy, however. This is because when emotions run high, things tend to go out of hand. But if you are willing to make an effort and put your mind to it, you can achieve anything you want to. On a lot of occasions, I have found out that the past plays a very big role in determining how you will react to pressure.

If you had been burned badly in the past, the actual thought of it occurring once again would send you jumping high to the mountains. You can try to avoid it for some time, but you are just delaying the inevitable. You will have to face the music in the end.

So, what can you do to handle conflict?

The first step is Just Breathe; you must learn the art of thinking before you act to calm yourself. In your mind, right now, I know you must be saying that it looks too simple an exercise to make a major difference. My advice to that is that you do not criticize an idea that you have not yet tried. If it is that simple, then you should have no problem setting aside a few minutes every day for it. Just look for someplace that is quiet and slowly take a breath in and out.

Clear your mind of negative thoughts because they just drain your energy. This is an art that takes some time to be perfect because you will constantly be tempted to think about what you need to do. To try to help these occurrences from happening, remind yourself that it takes only 5 minutes of your time to do it. When you get upset, or someone makes you angry, find a safe place, and count to 10 right away. This has been proven to be of great help and prevents you from saying things in the heat of the moment that you would later regret to have said.

Secondly, take action. Problems are not solved purely by thinking about them. Some action has to accompany it to make things happen. As soon as you have calmed your nerves, you must be willing to show that you have gotten past the fight and are looking for ways to remedy the situation. Think of possible solutions if it is something that keeps coming up.

Get some advice from your well-meaning friends. Should you need to confront a person about a certain issue, make sure that you do it with a clear mind. Avoid letting the situation turn violent. Be wary of the words that you use when you are dealing with your partner. Try to see where they are coming from as you tell them why you are hurt. It is good always to remember that if you plant kindness as a seed, you will harvest kindness in return.

Show Some Kindness; this is another method of showing your loved one that you are a good person despite the conflict. You may be asking yourself how this is related to your problems, but I assure you that when your loved one sees that you are attempting to be nice, you will feel more complete because they will acknowledge it. If you focus on the good side of a person, you will soon realize that your situation is not as bad as you thought it was and that other people are facing worse challenges.

It will help you realize that every couple has their fair share of challenges, and your relationship is not an exception to the rule. I have no better way of fueling your hope than to let you know that if you are willing to be better than the rest, you will be able to make a change for the better.

CHAPTER 12

THE ART OF PERSUASION

Within advertising, politics, and in general, any other area of daily life, persuasion is a skill that we must develop.

Many speak of it and recognize it as a weapon, probably if it is, but a weapon is within everyone's reach, and that is why I recognize persuasion as an art.

But why is persuasion an art that we should all develop?

I will give you an example that cannot fail:

The famous and scary job interviews... We all have to face them at some time in our lives.

Have you ever thought about why you didn't get to keep the position?

The first option may be that your profile was not what they were looking for. Your knowledge and skills were not necessary; in that case, you cannot do anything, but when the job description and you seem to be the same person, everything indicates that you will get the job. But when that doesn't happen, what went wrong?

Perhaps your speech was not good enough to persuade the interviewer and make him see that you are the piece that the company lacks.

Now, have you seen how persuasion is something that we all must learn?

But to continue talking about the subject, it is necessary that we first define what persuasion is, since it is also a concept that has different opinions and perceptions.

Aristotle is considered the father of Rhetoric, and he was the first to speak of persuasion. Rhetoric is nothing more and nothing less than the technique and art of speaking; remember that in Greek society oral trials and speeches predominated, which were perfected thanks to it.

So, persuasion is supported by good intention. It must be trustworthy and transparent and promote a positive benefit or impact; it does not manipulate as it is almost always thought.

It should be noted that in most cases, by not generalizing, the result is impacted by our beliefs and culture; however, persuasion can seek a good for both parties and not only for one, as our selfishness generally does.

Aristotle spoke to us about the existence of 3 pillars on which persuasion is based:

Pillars of persuasion

- **Ethos:** These arguments are of an affective and moral order and can be seen in the sender of the message. They appeal to the authority and credibility of who issues the speech, here the relationship with their audience is defined.
- **Pathos:** The pathos arguments are effective and are more related to the receiver of the message. We can remember that what changes people and causes a change in actions are emotions and not facts.
- **Logos:** Here, more reference is made to discourse itself. The arguments must be solid, appealing to the reason and intelligence of the audience. This is where the balance is found between emotional and analytical discourse.

In this way and leaving aside all these theoretical parts, let's talk about how persuasion influences advertising.

For this, we can approach persuasion from different angles and perspectives, such as consumer behavior, social influence, and design.

Surely when you think about advertising, the first thing that comes to your mind is manipulation and subliminal messages. But let me tell you that not everything works like this. Within the consumer, there are already certain patterns and beliefs that make them act in some way. The only thing that persuasion does is take advantage of these areas and accentuate the obvious.

What are the needs of consumers?

These personalities change from time to time, even daily, but we go a little further, to social influence.

When people belong to a group, new needs arise. Think about what were the needs that were created when you entered your current job?

For example, when people are promoted, they may no longer be able to get there by public transport, so they need to buy a car; maybe you also had to buy new clothes.

All these needs arise from a sense of belonging.

So here persuasion has pretty much won everything.

The need is already created and arriving at the store means that you must buy something, you only have to choose one option.

This is what we call consumer behavior; another example of this could be when you need to buy a new cell phone.

How is the purchase decision made?

Let us take the example of Apple; within its range of products it has three types of phones: cheap, medium and expensive.

When you get to the store, the seller shows you the first option, and you think "It is very expensive."

And then the second option is the cheapest ...

But when you know its price, this comes to mind: "It is cheaper, surely it has some error."

Finally, the third option is the most expensive, and you know that you definitely cannot buy it, so you end up buying the first option, which was the medium.

This purchase is closely linked to the beliefs we have as a society, and we always think that if it is cheap, then it is not so good.

Here is part of what you take advantage of when

creating a sales strategy, but that does not mean that "brands want to sell you the most expensive."

Regarding the persuasive design, the information must be presented clearly and pleasantly, without being so pretentious. Also, depending on what you want to show, different technical and visual resources must be used, all to make the user feel comfortable, and you can have a good memory of the experience you had. This is where we put into practice the pillars of Aristotle, and you must manage emotions, arguments, and give confidence to the public you are addressing. The goal is achieved when you generate a memory in the consumer's mind.

Remember that persuasion is not only used by speakers or politicians in their speeches; this is a skill that we all must develop to achieve things and the common good.

Do you remember Emma Watson's speech at the UN?

It is persuasive! And she advocates not only for an objective or benefit for her but for that of the world.

For work, a raise, at school, with your partner and with your family... persuasion is everywhere, put it into practice!

If you start creating persuasive designs, your brand will surely be more successful in terms of positioning it in the minds of consumers.

The History of Persuasion

Do you know what they have in common; a speech by Barack Obama, an announcement by Chanel, a gamification campaign for the VW Polo, and a press release by Repsol? The answer is found in work written more than 2,300 years ago! Its title is The Rhetoric and the author, Aristotle. This treaty establishes the foundations of corporate advertising, political, institutional, emotional, and journalistic communication.

Through this section, I will try to discover how the theoretical precepts and the methodology exposed in The Rhetoric are applied daily and in a multidisciplinary way in the areas of professional communication. The conceptual basis of the work revolves around the command of the word and discourse—discursiveness—as instruments to exercise persuasive communication. Along with these elements are the arguments or reasoning that will be presented to the public to convince them by appealing to their feelings and emotions. Likewise, Aristotle determines and analyzes the protagonists of this process: sender, receiver, message, and channel or medium. The issue is you must project an image of credibility, authority, and moderation that facilitates the acceptance of your messages by the interlocutor. As for the recipient, it will be essential to know their approximate age and social status. In this way, the contents will be adapted to the particularities of the audience. A persuasive message is characterized by a simple style but elaborate, not conveying the feeling of artificiality. The vocabulary will be clear and intelligible for all audiences. And the use of 'linguistic' resources that attract the attention of the interlocutor will be pertinent. Aristotle defines the structure of the messages in preamble, proposition, and epilogue. The preamble will capture the attention of the public to present the topic that will be addressed later. In the proposition, all the argumentative and narrative forces of the exhibition will be overturned. The epilogue will contain a synopsis to summarize and consolidate the transmitted message. The message will appeal to the rational and emotional component that predisposes the interlocutor in a sense desired by the sender. Finally, it specifies that the message and its structures will always be adapted to the channel or medium through which it is transmitted.

As a result, this section constitutes a look at the past that takes us back to the original concepts of communication. This appeal is relevant in the prevailing digital environment in which we are located. In fact, at present, we use the infinite number of technological supports and channels that are within our reach. Thus, we are present in traditional social networks (Facebook, Twitter, Instagram, Pinterest, YouTube, etc.) and other emerging ones (Periscope, Meerkat). And we are up to date with private messaging systems like Telegram and innovative applications like Snapchat. Of course, we know the trends in the creation of branded content (storytelling, scroll telling, etc.) And we try to approach the public through personalized, gamified, and quality themes, thus developing the cross-cutting nature of the information. But, simultaneously, we must not forget that the means—technological support—is not the end but must be a tool in the exercise of our profession. And we must remember the assertion of the classical thinkers: 'the oldest is the most modern.' Past and present shake hands, since the final objective—to guide, influence the interlocutor's will using persuasive stimuli and appealing to his emotions—continues to be the same twenty-three centuries later.

Persuasion 101

The Latin word "persuasĭo" came to our language as persuasion, the procedure, and the result of persuading. That Latin word, in turn, derives from a cultism, the verb "persuadere," which is made up of two elements: the prefix "per-," which means "completely," and the verb "suadere," which is synonymous to "advise."

This action (persuade) consists of convincing a person of something, using different motives, or appealing to different techniques.

For example: "First we are going to bet on persuasion: if we do not succeed, we will use force," "It does not serve to impose things with violence, it is essential to achieve persuasion," "Hours and hours of the talk were necessary for the persuasion of my parents, but finally I got permission, and I will be able to travel. "

Persuasion is accomplished through influence. The intention is that a subject modifies his way of thinking or his behaviors, for which it is necessary to influence him through his feelings or by supplying him with certain information that, until now, he did not know.

Persuasion can be said to be the opposite of coercion or imposition. While persuasion is accomplished by suggesting things, coercion and imposition are accomplished by force. This means that a person, when persuaded, will act as the other intends but on his own, without fear of a violent or repressive reaction.

Several factors contribute to persuasion. The common thing is usually to appeal to the commitment of the people, convincing them that what is proposed to them is the right thing. The position of the person trying to persuade another is also relevant. If the individual in question is an authority or is popular, his views are likely to have more persuasive power than the views of others. That is why many political parties bet on bringing celebrities as candidates in election processes.

To persuade someone, it must be taken into account that there are various methods, the most significant of which are the following:

-Emotional. Within this group, techniques such as seduction, pity, faith, tradition are used...

-Rational. In this case, recourse is made to proof, rhetoric, the establishment of arguments or logic, among others.

-Polemics. such as torture, mind control, and even brainwashing.

Nor can we overlook the existence of a well-known novel that chooses to be titled with the term in question. We are referring to Jane Austen's "Persuasion" (1816) (1775 - 1817), known for other works such as "Pride and Prejudice" (1813) or "Sense and Sensibility" (1811).

Specifically, "Persuasion" is the last book the English author wrote. It involves a protagonist Anne, a woman who suffered, due to social norms, a hard blow to love when she had to reject the man she was in love with, simply because she did not come from a wealthy family. That circumstance meant that she watched the years go by on her own. However, everything changes when she meets that man again, who is now a highly recognized and also enriched captain.

Discover When You Are the Target

Are you the puppet of others? Learn the three steps to cut the threads that bind you to those who try to handle you...

I don't understand how it happens, but every time I meet my sister, I lose. When Lidia wants me to do something for her, she always succeeds! Again, I don't know how it happens, but does the situation unfold in a way that leaves me no choice but to do what she wants?

This is Francis' complaint; Lidia, his older sister, is a teacher in the art of manipulation. And Francis is not alone; his sister's name can be substituted for a son, a husband, a mother-in-law, a colleague, or even a best friend. And there are people who, to get away with it, handle others as if they were puppets.

The manipulators, those skilled "puppeteers," know how to handle the strings of those who fall into their orbit to achieve their goals. Some do it consciously because their plan is coldly calculated; others act like this because it is the only way they know to get away with it. But everyone, without exception, can continue to work that way because they have a great partner. Guess who? The person who lets himself be manipulated. In many cases, she is not a victim, but a volunteer in that frustrating game. In other words: manipulation happens and persists because the manipulated allows it to happen.

Review your case. Perhaps you give in out of grief, out of a sense of obligation, because you fear offending that person or keeping the peace. Many times you feel that the circumstances have conspired in a way that leaves you no choice but, once again, to dance to the music you are playing (the most typical case is the vendor who warns you to act now! because the "wonderful" offer ends in five minutes). You end up feeling frustrated, irritated, exhausted, and full of resentment. The truth is that your relationships with these "puppeteers" are not the best. Also, how much time, money, resources, and peace of mind have you lost in the hands of the manipulators!

But is there a light at the end of this tunnel? The good news is that while you are responsible for what happens, in the same way, you can take control of your life and cut the threads that tie you to the manipulator. Here are three steps to achieve it.

1. Recognize the Game

Some victims of manipulation feel uncomfortable after dealing with one of these specimens but cannot identify exactly why. As Francis says, "I don't know how, but my sister always gets me to do what she wants."

That is why the first step to cut the threads that tie you to the manipulator is to recognize what their game is. In other words: discover what weapons he uses to wield you. Do they employ the penalty? "I have not had as good luck in life as you." Maybe they control you with guilt feelings. "If you don't help me, my children—your nephews!—will go bankrupt." Or he presents you with the fait accompli, believing that "it is better to ask for forgiveness than to ask permission." Example: "I took the liberty of taking this from your home." You must know their strategies so that you are prepared and not taken by surprise. "I discovered that my sister's tactic is to use the penalty." Does she play the unhappy, plagued by bad luck? "And I always fall," admits Francis. Once you recognize this person's modus operandi, take the next step.

2. Discover Your «Buttons»

Manipulators have an effective secret: they use the appropriate tactics for each person because they know which one works with each individual. With one is the feeling of guilt, while with another it is a pain; with some, it is vanity (the manipulator pretends to be incompetent to be rescued, making the rescuer feel important - without realizing that he has been used) or even fear of divorce, dismissal, abandonment or ruin.

What is your Achilles heel? Discover the «buttons» that you have, and that press you to operate as if you were a robot. When you determine that you always fall out of grief, vanity, or because you don't know how to act when you are presented with a fait accompli, stop. Discuss why you have that particular "button" and what your fear is if you don't budge. Are they realistic? Or are you allowing yourself to be influenced by the "puppeteer"? Is it fair to yourself that you feel influenced by the "puppeteer? And that you think like this? How does it affect you or harm you? And what effect does it have on your relationship with that person? Do you want to keep the threads that bind you to the «puppeteer»? If you want to cut them and be free, continue to the next step.

3. Modify Your Behavior

Now that you know what tactics these people use to manipulate you and you recognize why you fall into the trap; you should modify your behavior.

-Recognize tampering

-Don't be rushed. Take all the time you need to assess the situation and determine how you want to respond.

-Mentally prepare yourself for everything you will feel in those moments: grief, fear, guilt, and anxiety. Let those feelings flood you and pass, like a wave that envelops you and then drifts away. Remember: the "puppeteer" uses them precisely because they are effective. Accept the possibility that some people will stray from you or that some relationships will radically change. But if you are clear that nothing based on manipulation is positive, you will be at peace with that possibility.

-Express your preference or your position with kindness, but with total firmness. If the person insists, be consistent, since it is you who will teach others how they can be with you, simply by the treatment you allow. Be prepared to repeat the same thing a thousand times, and for the "puppeteer" to find other tactics to handle you. Again: be consistent. The moment you stop accepting manipulation, the person will understand that their tactics do not work for you - and you will be free.

When You Should Seek Help

Sometimes the situation reaches levels that you cannot handle using the same tactics that would work in normal situations. If you are dealing with an unstable person, physically abusing you, threatening suicide, or acting "crazy," take that situation very seriously and seek help urgently. Both you and others affected must be safe from a dangerous situation.

Behavioral Traits of Manipulation

If you still do not know how to identify a manipulative person, certain tips can help you.

These types of people usually have some characteristics that make them evident, so you must know what they are.

The dangerous thing about manipulative people is that they do not usually have any kind of scruples. When they detect a potential victim, they immediately search for their vulnerabilities to exploit them and take advantage of them through emotional manipulation.

This is done gradually; gradually enveloping people with words and acts of pretended empathy, which are only tools they use to achieve their nefarious purposes.

Although we are aware of the damage that a manipulator can bring to our lives, it is not an easy task to identify them and detect if we are facing any of them.

Fortunately, some fairly clear indications give them away, and to which we must remain vigilant, to avoid falling into their networks and to escape in time from their bad influences.

Traits that reveal a manipulative person

These are the most common behavioral traits that manipulative people present:

1. They are skilled speakers

Manipulators effectively handle the gift of speech.

They spin everything with great skill and always at their convenience, managing to dupe their victim through the distortion of ideas and their emotional exploitation.

All their activity is focused on mastering the situation and obtaining benefits or some type of performance; it always consists of their victims.

To do this, they purposely create a power imbalance; that allows them to exploit the other person without this fact being evident to their victim.

2. They are never satisfied

The manipulative person is not easily satiated and is always asking and squeezing incessantly.

His behavior has more to do with the satisfaction of his ego, through which he achieves the total manipulation of his victim.

This makes him feel that he has absolute control over her and that he can exploit her at his whim until he reaches the limit, demanding more and more until he achieves the emotional breakdown.

3. Impersonating a victim

This is the preferred role that is often played flawlessly by the manipulator.

It is a kind of emotional blackmail in which the manipulator turns out to be the victim and you the victimizer.

They proclaim that their situation is due to the bad behavior of other people and that they are the target of their injustices.

With this behavior, they manage to awaken people's sense of pity.

4. Present a picture of being needy

The manipulators present themselves as a weak person of spirit, who urgently requires support and is dependent on others.

But behind that lamb mask is a manipulative wolf, who exploits your good feelings until you feel responsible for his person; this is just a tactic to know how you act.

5. Lies easily

He has an extraordinary capability to lie, without being revealed by any gesture or the tone of his voice. He is a myth maniac with all the letters.

The level is such that in some cases, he becomes convinced of his lies, which makes them even more credible.

That is the reason why he turns to his victim at all stages of the manipulation process until he reaches his goals.

Lacking scruples, he tries to make one believe that his lies are not important and that they were not told with malicious intent, when these are evident.

Details you should not miss

For a manipulator to exist, there must also be a manipulated victim. If you allow a manipulator to recreate his tricks on you, he will have the fertile ground to launch his nets.

Manipulators completely devalue their victims, so it is necessary to avoid living with them at all costs.

CHAPTER 13

HOW TO RECOGNIZE DOUBLE-FACED PEOPLE

Double-faced people have both a private and a public face. Depending on the situation, they use different masks to harness opportunism to their banner. They pretend to be what they are not, to take advantage of it. In general, to receive social approval, or to place themselves above others. Did you know that Hypocritical people are sometimes called double-faced people?

Relationships are always challenging with a fake person since we're never sure what they think or feel. They certainly have no doubts about exploiting us to achieve their goals.

Hypocritical People: Definition.

Hypocrisy is confusion in what is being said and what is being done, or between what one thinks and feels and what is being portrayed. It is a way to hide or suppress true desires, thoughts, and emotions and instead, adapt to environmental expectations.

The word hypocrisy derives from an ancient Greek word, hupokrisis, which means "step." In that sense, a hypocrite, or hupokrités, was merely an actress, someone on stage pretending to be someone else.

But perhaps the best description of hypocrisy comes from American politician Adlai E. Stevenson, who said: "A hypocrite is the sort of individual who would cut a redwood, set up a stage, and then make a speech about nature preservation."

We all indeed experience a crucial tension as social beings between our interests and the interests of others. The desires cannot always coincide with those of others. To solve this conflict without renouncing our "I," and without causing undue social tension, we are developing different, more, or less assertive strategies that allow us to combine public and private interests.

There are individuals, however, who have not developed such techniques but tend to hide what they think or feel. It is not about people who are dependent or submissive, but they resort to hypocrisy as a tactic to achieve their goals. At the same time, it is a maladaptive tactic in the long run as it produces a deep dissonance between actions and feelings, values, and ideas.

How do you unmask the wrong person? Here are Double-faced people's top five behaviors:

1. They are happy to see someone punished. Their "high" moral norm causes them to point the accusing finger at someone, and it is not uncommon for them to humiliate or disqualify someone even in public. It's a retaliation tactic in which they seek to concentrate attention on the other's perceived mistakes, failures, or flaws so that those around them don't know their differences and hypocrisy.

2. They have an aura of moral arrogance. Double-faced people appear to be halfway between narcissism and moral dominance. We are also victims of the Dunning-Kruger effect, and the level of arrogance will make us feel low-level, inexperienced when we communicate with them, or we may just assume that we are not good enough.

3. They never get the rules. There are laws and regulations, but they apply only to others. Hypocrites assume that they are above the law because they have an inherent sense of justice and morality and are not obligated to obey it.

4. The blame is never theirs, and they always have an excuse. Double-faced people typically do not notice their conflicts and errors, even though they are really clear. Such people do not apologize or accept their guilt, and they are continually resorting to excuses. Circumstances are always mitigating for them, and mistakes never belong.

5. Do what I'm saying and not what I am doing. This may be the maxim that guides hypocrites. Their acts rarely align with the underlying beliefs of their expression or attitudes. This is because their primary incentive is to look nice and make the best of it for others.

The three tactics Double-faced and Fake people use

1. Moral double standards. It refers to hypocritical individuals who invoke irreproachable motivations on an ongoing basis but who do not personally behave according to those moral laws. For example, a person may continually speak about the importance of helping others, but they look the other way when the time comes to reach out to those who need support. Or a person who praises ideals such as honesty and the importance of telling the truth, but then his wife becomes unfaithful.

2. Equal moral principles. This applies to false people who are soft when it comes to self-judgment but apply a strict moral norm to others. For example, if a driver doesn't stop when he gets to a crosswalk, the pedestrian will be really upset, but when this pedestrian is behind the wheel and doing the same, he will use reasons to justify why he did not stop. He's the one who can see the speck in another's eye but not the log in his own eye.

3. Moral frailty. There are individuals who, due to cognitive dissonance, contradict their own attitudes. For instance, a person may talk about the importance of going to vote, but he doesn't go to the polls on voting day. In this scenario, what fails is self-control. The individual believes what he says, but he doesn't have enough courage when it comes to putting it into action. However, he doesn't want to admit it publicly and continues to offer moral lessons.

How are we so double-faced?

You probably know more than one Double-faced person in your world. And you're probably still wondering how you could seem unaware of the tension between his words and his act. The theory for this phenomenon comes from psychologist Patricia Linville who worked at Yale University, and the word "self-complexity" was coined in the mid-1980s. Their theory is that the less complex the "I" cognitive representation is, the more severe the variations in the mood and attitudes of the individual would become.

In other words, some people seem to view themselves from a very narrow viewpoint. For example, they define themselves by the positions they perform, so they think they're a "self-sacrificing mother" or a "good boss." The issue is that having such a restricted self-definition makes us mentally more dysfunctional and prevents us from coping with the contradictions inherent in ourselves.

We will take a look at an experiment performed at the University of Miami to understand this phenomenon better. Psychologists asked college students to determine the value of research competencies. They were then asked to recall all the occasions they had ignored the report, intending to unmask the potential hypocrisy behind the initial responses.

Interestingly, students who had less self-complexity at that time were more likely to change their initial opinions; that is, they rectified suggesting that learning was not so necessary after all.

This could clarify why some people are saying one thing and doing another. Their remarks come from a completely different portrayal of the "me" in certain situations acting on the "me." In practice, double-faced people are only trying to keep the identity simple, and they have built up immunity by separating their words from their actions.

For example, in the case of politicians, it is normal for them to hold a conversation related to their "political self," while doing something diametrically opposite in their "job" or "family" life. They try to preserve their separate "selves" in this way, so they cannot combine them.

Such reports indicate that many people have double-faced faces without knowing it. In reality, they sometimes fail to understand and hide behind excuses when we bring them face to face with their contradictions.

Not everyone lives in this "hypocritical ignorance" society. Some learn to manipulate hypocrisy, particularly when they understand that it is neither practical nor beneficial to pursue those ideas. Such people have no trouble announcing something and doing the opposite only because they think it's more convenient. Yet neither do they publicly accept their hypocrisy because it is too humiliating and would be a major blow to their "I," which is why they argue that circumstances have changed them.

How do Double-faced men trouble us so much?

The response comes from research conducted at Yale University or at least part thereof. Psychologists have discovered that what most disturbs us about Double-faced is not the incoherence between their words and their acts, but rather that their moral proclamations are misleading and tend to appear as more upright people than they are.

We don't like hypocrites in reality, because they trick us. Also, it has been shown that we tend to accept and support moral claims or that to justify the actions implies a certain degree of generalization. For example, if a person leaves a project, we prefer the reason, "There is no point in spending more energy" than "I don't want to spend more energy." And when we come across the truth, we feel more disappointed and discouraged.

That means we are also contributing to the hypocrisy that persists on a social level, in a way. In reality, we might have acted in a Double-faced manner, even in other circumstances, to try to give us a better picture of ourselves.

How to deal with Double-faced people?

Being truthful and recognizing that many inconsistencies coexist within each of us is the best way to combat hypocrisy. In certain circumstances, we can all act hypocritically, but there is an important line between the level of social and tolerable hypocrisy and the intolerable hypocrisy which pretends to offer moral lessons. We don't have to meet other people's expectations, nor do we have to become morals preachers. We just have to live and let live.

Hear him out. While a Double-faced person's first response to criticism is to become angry, the smart thing to do is to calm down and listen. His words may well stem from genuine concern for us. And we have to learn to distinguish the grain from the chaff, and we will consider it if the idea is worth it. If it is not, then we should still disregard it.

Don't beat him up. It is typically futile to explicitly accuse a Double-faced person of not practicing what he preaches because it will produce a defensive reaction. Oddly enough, that person will respond by counterattacking, falling into an argument that makes no sense to figure out who is the less hypocritical of both. Therefore, no matter how much his words annoy you, do not lose composure, and do not strike him. Remember that you are influenced by who makes you mad.

Don't feel bad about it. The hypocritical person would probably make you feel bad for not being good enough. When you are aware of the reasons for your actions, it is important that you retain perspective and do not feel guilty. Remember that it can only damage you, to which you add undue importance, after all.

Conversation explains. In certain cases, double-faced people go around the bush, spreading a general and ambiguous argument in which everyone is guilty and immoral, but in particular, they do not point the accusing finger at anybody. If you think, in his voice, he refers to you, ask him if he is. It's just enough to ask for a clarification of his vocabulary to put a stop to his attitude.

Mark your boundaries. If the hypocrite crosses your red lines, then feel free to mark them. You should let him know you are not going to tolerate moral discourses or undeserved rebukes that make you feel bad. Speak quietly and with certainty. If the Double-faced person realizes that his discourse does not make an impression on you, he will leave you alone sooner rather than later.

CHAPTER 14

DARK PERSUASION METHODS

In Aristotle's Rhetoric, logos is the most prominent type of rhetoric. It refers to logical reasoning, to our attempt to make use of the intellect.

When we present our arguments, whether oral or written, we try to be persuasive. Just before accepting our claims, the public must consider our point of view. That is what rhetoric is; that others adopt our point of view.

So, who better to explain the rhetoric than Aristotle? Plato's student studies focused on rhetoric. For this reason, Aristotle's rhetoric consists of three categories: pathos, ethos, and logos.

In Aristotle's rhetoric, pathos, ethos, and logos are the three fundamental pillars. Today, these three categories are considered different ways of convincing an audience about a particular topic, belief, or conclusion. Let's delve into the topic below.

Aristotle's pathos

Pathos means 'suffering and experience.' In Aristotle's rhetoric, this carries over to the speaker or writer's ability to evoke emotions and feelings in his audience. The pathos is associated with emotion, appeals to empathize with the audience, and spark your imagination.

Essentially, pathos is seeking empathy with the audience. When used, the argument's values, beliefs, and understanding are engaged and communicated to the audience through a story. Thus, according to studies such as those carried out at Nijmegen University in Norway by doctors Frans Derkse and Jozien Bensing, empathy is key to improving not only communication but the connection between people from an emotional point of view.

The pathos is used when the arguments to be presented are controversial. Since these arguments are often lacking in logic, success will reside in the ability to empathize with the audience.

In a case for constitutionally banning abortion, for instance, the descriptive language may be used to depict babies and the promise of a fresh beginning to elicit sorrow and fear on the part of the public.

Aristotle's ethos

The second category, ethos, means character and comes from the word ethnos, which means moral and showing moral personality. For speakers and writers, the ethos is shaped by its credibility and similarity to the audience. As an authority on the subject, the speaker must be trustworthy and respected.

It is not enough to allow rational justification for the arguments to be successful. To appear trustworthy, information has to be delivered accurately, as well.

Ethos is especially important in generating popular interest, according to Aristotle's rhetoric. The message sound and style would be crucial to that.

Furthermore, the character is also going to be influenced by the speaker's reputation, which is independent of the message.

For example, speaking to an audience as an equal, rather than as passive characters, increases the likelihood that people will engage in actively listening to arguments.

Aristotle's logos

Logos means word, speech, or reason. Convincingly, the logos is the rationale behind claims by the author. The logos refer to every effort and logical arguments to speak to the intellect. Thus, logical reasoning presents two forms: deductive and inductive.

Deductive reasoning argues that, "If A is true, and B is true, the intersection of A and B must also be true."

For example, the logos argument of "women like oranges" would be "women like fruits" and "oranges are fruits."

Inductive reasoning also uses premises, but the conclusion is only an expectation and may not necessarily be true because of its subjective nature. For example, the phrases "Peter likes comedy" and "This movie is a comedy" can reasonably conclude that "Peter will like this movie."

Aristotle's rhetoric

In Aristotle's rhetoric, logos was his favorite argumentative technique. However, on a day-to-day basis, everyday arguments depend more on pathos and ethos. The combination of all three is used to make rehearsals more persuasive and central to the discussion team's strategy.

The people who master them have the ability to convince others to perform a certain action or to buy a product or service. Even so, in modernity, the pathos seems to have a greater influence. Populist discourses, which seek to excite rather than provide logical arguments, seem to be catching on more easily.

The same is true for fake news. Many may lack logic, but, despite their strong capacity to empathize, the public embraces them. Being aware of these three techniques in Aristotle's rhetoric will help us to understand certain arguments that are intended to convince us even by fallacies.

CHAPTER 15

NEURO-LINGUISTIC PROGRAMMING

It is easy for the concept of Neuro-linguistic Programming to generate confusion. What is it based on? When does it apply? Here are some key ideas to know what NLP is.

What is Neuro-linguistic Programming?

Steve Bavister and Amanda Vickers (2014) define Neuro-linguistic Programming as a communication model that focuses on identifying and using thought models that influence a person's behavior as a way to improve the quality and effectiveness of life.

One problem with NLP is the nature of its name, since, when the term "Neuro-linguistic Programming" is mentioned to people who have never heard of it, the reaction is usually a bit negative. On the other hand, the name could suggest that we are dealing with empirical techniques derived from neuroscience, but no evidence confirms their efficacy.

Stephen Briers (2012) says that NLP is not a coherent treatment, but "a hodgepodge of different techniques without a very clear theoretical basis." This author maintains that the maxim of Neuro-linguistic Programming is narcissistic, egocentric, and dissociated from the notions of responsibility.

Also, he states that "sometimes we have to accept and mourn the death of our dreams, not only occasionally dismiss them as inconsequential. The re-framing of NLP puts us in the role of a widower avoiding the pain of mourning by jumping into a relationship with a younger woman, not stopping to say a proper goodbye to his dead wife. "

What does the Neuro-linguistic Programming model focus on?

The world is experienced through five senses: sight, hearing, touch, smell, and taste. Much information comes to us continuously; consciously and unconsciously, we eliminate what we do not want to pay attention to. We are told that the remaining information is based on our past experiences, values, and beliefs. What we end up with is incomplete and inaccurate, since some of the general information has been removed, and the rest has been generalized or distorted.

What is NLP based on?

The most important thing to have a vision of what

Neuro-Linguistic Programming is, is to know that it is based on four fundamental aspects, which are known as the "four pillars," according to Steve Bavister and Amanda Vickers (2014).

1. Results

To achieve something, we talk about objectives; in NLP, the term of results is used. If there is a prior concentration on what you want to achieve, there will be a guide that will guide all of that person's available resources toward achieving a goal.

2. Sensory acuity

Sensory acuity refers to the ability to observe or detect small details to be aware of what is happening around us. People vary greatly in realizing what they see, hear, or feel. Some people are dedicated to observing their environment more, while others are more focused on their own emotions and thoughts.

3. Flexibility in behavior

When you start to know what your results are and use your sensory acuity to observe what is happening, the information you obtain allows you to make adjustments in your behavior, if necessary. If the actions you perform don't take you in the direction you want, then you should obviously try to go another way or try something different. However, many people lack that flexibility in behavior and insist on doing the same thing over and over again.

4. Rapport

The rapport could be considered as that component that unites people. Most of the time, it happens naturally, automatically, instinctively. Some people we meet seem to share our life perspective, while there are other people we don't connect with. The capacity for rapport with other people must be improved to obtain more effective relationships.

The presuppositions of Neuro-linguistic Programming

Salvador Carrión (2008), refers that a presupposition is something we take for granted without any proof. It tells us that Neuro-linguistic Programming does not intend that the presuppositions are true, although there is quite palpable evidence to support many of them. I have tried to search for the "evidence" that supports these assumptions, but I have only found an explanation for each of them.

Life, mind, and body are one system

The mind and body are considered as a single system; each was directly influencing the other. For example, what happens inside your body affects your thoughts and will affect the people around you.

You can't stop communicating

The message we are trying to convey is not always the one that others receive. Therefore, from Neuro-linguistic Programming, it tells us that we must be aware of the reactions of others to see if our message has been successful. This can lead to serious difficulties when preparing a message, since focusing on reactions or being alert to possible consequences is not something that will add quality to communication.

Beneath each behavior, there is a positive intention

In addiction or bad behavior, there is always a positive intention. Therefore finding the root of that problem and externalizing the positive intention, you can go from smoking for 15 years to not having that need.

If what you're doing doesn't work, do something else

If you try a way to approach a problem and don't get the results you expected, try something different and keep varying your behavior until you get the answer you were looking for.

If one person can do something, everyone can learn to do it

There is, in NLP, the process of modeling excellence. If you want an article published, for example, you could look at someone who is brilliant at writing and imitate the way they do it. In this way, you will be immersing yourself in the knowledge of great value.

Criticism of New Language Programming

Roderique-Davies (2009) states that using the word "neuro" in NLP is "effectively fraudulent since NLP does not explain the neural level, and it could be argued that its use is falsely fed on the notion of scientific credibility."

On the other hand, Devilly (2005) maintains that the so-called "power therapies" gain popularity because they are promoted, like other pseudoscience's, using a set of tactics of social influence. These include making extraordinary claims such as "a one-session cure for any traumatic memory." These types of strategies are incredibly disproportionate and play with the health of many people who place their trust in professionals with supposed preparation and ethics when carrying out their activity.

The few effective tools or more or less proven theories of Neuro-linguistic Programming, do not belong exclusively to it, and what is new has not been empirically proven. What's more, what's new about it, either seems very simplistic or contradicts what science says.

Verbal vs. Non-Verbal Communication

NLP uses both verbal and non-verbal language. Rapport can be established both through the verbal language as the non-verbal. The meaning of communication is the verbal and non-verbal response we receive. By understanding the power of non-verbal language, we can realize that rather than investing in word management, it is much better to invest in the control of our internal states and to make our verbal language consistent with non-verbal language.

The interlocutor's unconscious psyche will capture the discrepancy between verbal and non-verbal language. Observing the non-verbal language of others is very interesting. NLP supporters, by way of example, argue that through aspects of nonverbal language such as eye movement, we can discover if someone is cheating.

For this, you must take into consideration, apart from your sensitive state, the other person's channel, the connection, the verbal language (not just words), and your non-verbal language. This is a tool to have a better understanding of what people do essentially through the language and observation of their non-verbal language. Neuro-linguistic programming is the science that takes care to study the mental patterns of each person.

The moment a person cheats, their non-verbal language runs counter to their words, if we are careful to capture their non-verbal language. Calibrating a person means knowing, through their non-verbal and verbal language, their internal state. That is, their state of mind and taking it into account in the communication process.

This form of internal representation is reflected in the way of meditating, the verbal and non-verbal language used, the movement of the eyes, the physiology, the genre of breathing, the timbre of the voice, etc. Words can disguise thoughts and feelings, but the body does not so that in the case of dissonance between verbal and non-verbal language, one is going to have to adhere to what is communicated by the body. We already know that NLP is the science of how language, verbal, and non-verbal, affects the neurological system.

However, the best way to notice our partner's lies is to observe non-verbal language. The non-verbal language alone is not an impact tool, but is an addition.

Verbal (words spun with logic and cohesion)

Non-Verbal (gestures, postures, movements, tone, etc.)

For example, for a politician speaking, it is not so essential precisely what is stated, but rather the emphasis he places through gestures and changes in voice modulation.

Learn to notice inconsistencies between verbal language and the anatomical can be very useful for you. Words and verbal language are largely a selective summary of what is going on in our heads. What we know by persuasion is an NLP model that affirms to us that through the superficial structure, which is a verbal and non-verbal language, we can get to know the deep structure, that is, the internal representations of our interlocutor.

NLP To Influence

You are constantly influencing others. Maybe that surprises you, but it's true. Here's why.

Language does not allow us to embrace and express all of reality at once. Choosing your words is necessary to exclude others. Choosing your words also means limiting the immense wealth of your thoughts. What you communicate thus necessarily orientates in one direction or another. Therefore, communication is inseparable from influence.

That is why in NLP, it is said that it is impossible not to influence. Without you being necessarily aware of it, each of your words, each of your actions is capable of having an impact on others (by frightening them, destabilizing them, or by convincing them, inspiring them, motivating them).

It remains to be seen which way you want to influence.

Influencing others does not mean manipulating others. It is entirely possible to broaden your sphere of influence with ethics. You exercise manipulation when you turn fully to your personal goal without taking into consideration the interests of the individuals involved. This might surprise you, but you are unconsciously constantly influencing others, especially when you choose your words to communicate and exclude others. What you express necessarily leads to some meaning. So, you can't talk about influence without talking about communication. In NLP, it is said that it is impossible to perform acts or speak without impacting on something or a person. But all your gestures and your words are not necessarily emitted with a conscience. You can learn to convince, to be the source of inspiration for those around you, to motivate your colleagues to influence with NLP. Read on to find out how.

Methods to influence with NLP

Now that you know the difference between manipulating and influencing NLP, you will be able to ethically impact the behavior of others without focusing solely on your cause. It remains to be seen for what purpose you wish to do this. Below you will find a set of methods to apply daily. These will also allow you to make good use of your sales, seduction, or persuasion skills.

Influencing with NLP and foot in the door

The "foot in the door" method consists, first of all, of asking for a small service that no one can refuse, then demanding a more important one.

Example: you ask your neighbor to empty your mailbox during your absence. This person accepts, then before leaving, you also ask him to water your plants, he cannot refuse you after accepting the first service.

Influencing with NLP or the door in the nose

Unlike the foot-in-the-door technique, the door in the nose is asking a person for a service that they cannot do. The influencer knows this, but behind this request, he will propose something much more acceptable.

Example: You are influenced by the "door in your nose" when your boss asks you to work this weekend. He knows that you will refuse this request and has planned something else. He then suggests that you work more than 8 hours next Monday. It will be impossible for you to have to say "no" again.

Influencing with NLP and priming

"Priming" is not a technique of influence, but rather of manipulation. It should not be used if your goal is not to manipulate others. One feels the lie by playing on the incompleteness of the information.

Example: You have seen on the Internet that a store offers cheap clothing. When you arrive, the vendors tell you that these items are sold out, when in reality they only wanted you to come to spend more money than you expected when you saw something that you liked. These inexpensive clothes never existed.

Foot to mouth technique

The foot-in-the-mouth technique uses formulas of interrogative politeness to obtain positive responses until the end of the conversation.

Example: To get a positive response from a healthy person, you will ask them, "How are you?" » « "Do you like the weather?" » And so on until asking him, « "Would you like to go there and eat some good ice cream?"

Influencing with NLP or fear-relief

The fear-relief system consists of causing great anxiety by indirectly making threats. Then the person who tries to influence will change his tone after a while by the presence of an associate. The person who has suffered the fear will suddenly relieve it. This relief will instinctively push him to submit to expectations. Doesn't that remind you of your couple's arguments?

The "forearm touch" method

This technique may surprise you, but you can try it to find out. It turns out that touching a person's forearm without provoking them while avoiding that person's gaze allows you to obtain what you expect from this individual very easily.

The participation

Even the smallest participation allows you to get what you want. Commit as long as possible because it will change the image that others had of you. Little effort can be enough to impact many things.

Emotionally classify people

When you rank someone for what they do well, you will touch their heart. Tell him that he is orderly when you see his room well cleaned and furnished. Unconsciously, he will spend more hours cleaning this space in the future.

Support your statement with well-chosen words; for example, "it shows that you like taking care of people."

NLP Techniques You Must Master

We have heard of them, but what are NLP techniques? Indeed, we cannot speak of Neuro-linguistic Programming as a science, which is why it has received some criticism. But it is considered a "model," that is, a set of techniques and theories focused on understanding behaviors and orienting the human being towards self-knowledge and the achievement of objectives.

But better, let's first analyze its acronyms carefully:

On the one hand, we have the word "programming," which refers to the intention to reprogram psychological behaviors, beliefs, and processes. The concept "neuro" leads us to the idea that all behavior is based on a series of neurological processes. And finally, "linguistics" responds to the concept that all these neurological processes are expressed through a specific verbal and body language.

NLP is a set of models, skills, and techniques to think and act effectively in the world. The purpose of NLP is to be useful, increase options, and improve quality of life.

-John Grinder-

NLP principles And Techniques, You Must Master

That dimensional triad that we mentioned has the initial objective of understanding our internal processes to reprogram the way we communicate and express ourselves, to change beliefs, and to make us feel safe to achieve our success. Quite a challenge, right? But let's get to know, in a brief way, some more of its aspects and NLP techniques.

1. Communication

NLP tells us that the way we communicate and the words we use define our reality and the way we understand the world. A personal perspective that sometimes does not coincide with that of our interlocutors.

In addition to this, people have two types of communication: internal (what we think and feel within ourselves) and external (where in addition to the words that we express aloud, gestures, postures and gestures are united).

2. How to process information

We differentiate ourselves in our way of "capturing" information. Some people are guided more by the visual, others by the auditory route, others by the sensations... Stop for a moment on this idea: How do you remember things the most, with words or images?

Try to remember a moment from your past; how does that memory come to mind? Observe how you analyze and capture the information around you, if you are, for example, more visual or auditory.

3. The anchor

A way to achieve objectives or overcome certain problems would be based on this concept, already used by behavioral psychology and one of the basic NLP techniques.

Let's imagine a situation that causes us a lot of anguish and anxiety; public speaking, for example. One way to deal with this reality would be to "anchor" a pleasant, relaxed, and positive moment of our memory and associate it using visualization and breathing techniques with the "stressful situation."

A walk on the beach when we were children, a sunset with our partner, relaxing music... all this should help us "weaken that fear" and reprogram new realities where harmony prevails. In this way, gradually, we "anchor" ourselves in a calm and pleasant situation to face an event that is stressful for us.

4. The time

Time is of particular importance for each person, but you must know how to manage yourself appropriately. In the past, our memories and emotions come together, a trunk from which good things can sometimes be taken to redirect the "now."

Because it is in the present where sensory experiences prevail, in which truly important events take place and where we must invest all our efforts given a good future. Therefore, working in the present is essential in NLP to sow the future that we would like to have.

The future does not yet exist; hence it must be established as that point where our desires are nailed to push our present. Our now.

5. Ecology of systems

We all have a system of beliefs and determined values built throughout our lives, and they are the motors that guide our neurological axes. "We are what we believe," and beliefs are the conceptions of our world, which promote action and behavior.

Sometimes these beliefs are so ingrained in our being that we do not even realize if they are beneficial for us or not. We may be hurting ourselves without knowing it... Hence, NLP delves into our ecology of systems to make us aware and reorganize these structures more beneficially and optimally.

These are then, in broad strokes, the basic pillars on which this approach to the human mind is based. Neuro-linguistic Programming, where the way we interpret our reality and organize the information prevails: the senses, the language, the time, words, memories, beliefs... are those leaves that make up the tree of our life.

NLP techniques help to vary or focus differently on some of these parts to direct our lives towards certain goals.

CHAPTER 16

BODY LANGUAGE 101

Body language: Body movements and learned or somatogenic gestures, non-oral, visual, auditory, or tactile perception, alone or about the linguistic and paralinguistic structure and the communicative situation. It may also be defined as the specific term used for modes of communication that include body movements and gestures, rather than (or beside) sounds, verbal language, or other types of communication. Body movements that bring special meanings to the spoken word during a communicative event can sometimes have an intention or not. These movements are studied by kinesics.

Developing

Sometimes a text is used instead of a word or a sentence, or something is drawn with the hands to complement what is said orally. For example, the signal of what is said goes between quotation marks which are made with the index and middle fingers of both hands. For example: to indicate late arrival, the clock is tapped. It belongs to the category of paralanguages, which describe all forms of non-verbal human communication. This includes the most subtle and unconscious movements, including winking and slight eyebrow movements. Also, body language can include the use of facial expressions and posture.

Paralanguage (including body language) has been extensively studied in social psychology. In everyday discourse and popular psychology, the term is often applied to body language considered involuntary. However, the difference between what is considered voluntary and involuntary body language is often controversial. For example, a smile can be triggered consciously or unconsciously.

Body posture

Body posture is the posture of the body or its parts about a reference system, either the orientation of an element of the body with another element or with the body as a whole, or its relationship with another person.

Within the body language, one talks about open or closed postures. The first ones are those postures where there are no barriers such as arms or legs between one interlocutor and others, otherwise in closed postures, where for example, crossed arms are used to isolate or protect the body (unconsciously in many cases). Furthermore, it is important to consider the ideal positions to speak according to the case, for example:

- In competitive situations: face to face
- To help or cooperate: next door
- To chat: at a right angle

Head posture

- Side to side movements: denial.
- Up and down movements: assent.
- Above: neutral or evaluation.
- Laterally tilted: interest.
- Tilt down: disapproval, negative attitude.

Arms pose

- Standard crossing: defensive posture, can also mean insecurity.
- Crossing them while keeping your fists closed indicates a sign of defense and hostility.
- Crossing your arms holding your arms is a sign of restriction.

Leg pose

- Standard crossing: defensive attitude.
- Cross in 4 ("in Indian"): competition, discussion.
- Cross while standing: discomfort, tension.
- Cross the ankles: used to conceal a negative attitude.

Important considerations

If you lean too much towards the other person, you will be invading their personal space. And this should not be done when there is still not much confidence, you will appear too aggressive.

Arms crossed are a sign. Keeping your arms crossed is a sign of withdrawal; it means that the person does not want to be intimate, that they do not feel confident, or that they are not completely well.

A shrunken posture means boredom.

Maintaining a relaxed position with slightly open arms and legs demonstrates self-confidence and security.

Getting closer than you should or a rigid body can demonstrate aggressiveness.

Showing yourself upright is the best thing for when you want to demonstrate security, courage, and importance in what you do.

Hands on the waist: defiance, aggressiveness.

Thumbs on the waist or pockets: manhood.

Finger-pointing: challenge.

The gestures

A gesture is a form of non-verbal communication executed with some part of the body and produced by the movement of the joints and muscles of the arms, hands, and head.

The language of gestures allows a variety of feelings and thoughts to be expressed, from contempt and hostility to approval and affection. Virtually all people use gestures and body language in addition to words when they speak. There are ethnic groups and certain communication languages that use many more gestures than the average. Certain types of gestures can be considered culturally acceptable or not, depending on the place and context in which they are performed. Five categories of gestures are distinguished, proposed by Paul Ekman and Wallace Friesen:

- **Emblematic gestures or emblems:** they are signals emitted intentionally and that everyone knows their meaning. (thumb raised)
- **Illustrative gestures:** gestures that accompany verbal communication to clarify or emphasize what is said, to impersonate a word in a difficult situation, etc. They are used intentionally. These gestures are very

useful in speeches and when speaking in public.

- **Regulatory gestures of interaction:** with them, communication is synchronized or regulated, and the channel does not disappear. They are used to take over in conversation, to start and end the interaction, to give way to speak... (shake hands).

- **Gestures that express emotional states or displays of affection:** this type of gesture reflects the emotional state of the person and is the emotional result of the moment. As an example, we can mention gestures that express anxiety or tension, grimaces of pain, triumph, joy, etc.

- **Adaptation or adapting gestures:** these are gestures that are used to manage emotions that are not wanted to be expressed. Here you can distinguish signs directed at oneself (such as pinching oneself), directed towards objects (pen, pencil, cigar, etc.) and those directed towards other people (such as protecting another person). Adapters can also be unconscious. Very clear examples are biting a fingernail or sucking a finger, very common in young children.

Facial expression

With facial expression, many moods and emotions are expressed. It is used to regulate interaction and to reinforce or emphasize the content of the message addressed to the recipient. The facial expression is used to express the mood, indicate attention, show disgust, joke, blame, reinforce verbal communication, etc. Paul Ekman developed a method to decipher facial expressions while working with Wallace Friesen and Silvan Tomkins. It is a kind of atlas of the face that is called FAST (Facial Affect Scoring Technique). FAST classifies images using photographs (not verbal descriptions) and dividing the face into three areas: the forehead and eyebrows, the eyes, and the rest of the face, that is, the nose, cheeks, mouth, and chin.

The look

The gaze is studied separately for its importance, although it is part of facial expression. The gaze fulfills a series of functions:

- The regulation of the communicative act.
- Source of information.
- Express emotions.
- Communicate the nature of interpersonal relationships.

The study of the gaze contemplates different aspects, among the most important of which we can mention: the dilation of the pupils, eye contact, the act of blinking, and the way of looking:

- The dilation of the pupils indicates interest and attractiveness, and they dilate when something interesting is seen.
- The number of times you blink per minute is related to calm and nervousness. If you blink a lot, it is a symbol of nervousness and restlessness, and the less you blink, the calmer you will be.
- Eye contact consists of the gaze that one person directs to the gaze of the other. Here we must mention the frequency with which we look at the other person and the maintenance of eye contact.
- The way of looking is one of the most relevant behaviors to distinguish high-status, dominant, and powerful people from low-status people who are not powerful.

The smile

Although the smile is included or can be included in the facial expression, it deserves to be explained in detail. It is used to express happiness, joy, or sympathy. The smile can even be used to make situations more bearable. It can have a therapeutic effect on pessimistic or depressed people.

- **Simple smile:** with this type of smile, an insecure, doubtful message of lack of confidence is transmitted. It should be avoided if you want to give an impression of firmness and confidence.
- **Simple smile of high intensity:** this smile occurs with a more pronounced separation of the corners of the mouth, and this rises more. A small part of the upper teeth can be seen. It transmits confidence and heat.
- **Upper Smile:** The upper lip retracts so that almost all or all of the teeth can be seen. A message of some satisfaction is transmitted by seeing someone.
- **Superior smile of high intensity:** it opens the mouth more, and the teeth are seen more. A light closure of the eyes usually accompanies it. Apart from conveying happiness, it is often used to say a happy question or to represent a funny surprise. It is often used deceptively; for this reason, care must be taken.
- **Wide smile:** it is one in which the gaze narrows slightly. The upper and lower teeth are fully exposed. This type of smile

expresses the highest intensity of joy, happiness, and pleasure.

- **Laughter:** it is the one that goes beyond the broad one. It is the most contagious and occurs in a group of people.

Make Body Language Your Superpower

It is common for tension to invade us in situations of pressure, such as taking exams, speaking in public, job interviews, etc. But did you know that you can easily manipulate your body chemistry to feel safer and more powerful? Studies indicate that you can achieve this simply by practicing certain changes in your body posture before undergoing stressful situations.

It is already known that our postures and gestures, often unconscious, communicate and allow others to have an idea of how we are or how we feel; this is called the body or non-verbal language.

Experts in the field of psychology and communication have devoted countless studies to understanding the effects of body language when looking for persuasive communication or a positive projection towards others. Still, Amy Cuddy, a specialist in social psychology at Princeton University, highlights that our body language not only influences how others see us but can determine how we feel (literally).

Cuddy explains that although the smile is the physical way in which we demonstrate the feeling of happiness, studies show that we can consciously provoke the same feeling of happiness by holding a pencil between our teeth and smiling for a few seconds. This means that not only does our mind dominate our body, but we can also use our body to manipulate our mental state.

According to these same studies, powerful people tend to have more positive, confident, and risky attitudes than non-powerful and insecure people, and this is reflected in their body language. While a secure person shows openness, the insecure person hides his body more in rigid and collected postures. Biologically we can find similar differences between the power poles, where the powerful have high levels of testosterone (hormone of domination) and low levels of cortisol (stress hormone). At the same time, insecure people show low levels of testosterone and high levels of cortisol.

Based on this relationship between our chemistry and our body language, Cuddy carried out several experiments to check whether taking different positions can affect our internal chemistry and, with this, consciously change how we feel.

The experiments consisted of taking different types of postures for 2 minutes and then taking saliva samples, gambling, and answering questions to determine the level of power/confidence one felt after adopting the two types of posture.

Results in individuals who adopted "High Power" positions:

- They decided to bet: 80%
- Testosterone level: 20% increase
- Cortisol level: Decrease by 25%

Results in individuals who adopted "Low Power" positions:

- They decided to bet: 60%
- Testosterone level: Decrease by 10%
- Cortisol level: 15% increase

The experiment showed amazing results, noting that with just 2 minutes of practicing the different postures, the internal chemistry of the body changed in significant percentages. This determined how individuals felt about themselves and influencing their attitude and decision-making.

A second experiment, which involved people practicing the same postures before a job interview, verified the positive effects of adopting "High Power" postures. This is because those who practiced these postures were more confident and assertive during their interviews, favoring their selection by 85%.

CHAPTER 17

HYPNOSIS 101

ANYONE can quickly and easily learn the techniques necessary to become a hypnotist. In any case, to become a good hypnotist, it is necessary to be upright, honest, and to dedicate oneself to this activity for humanitarian purposes. In the case of having all these qualities, the only thing you need is to memorize the techniques and then practice, practice, and more practice to continue learning every time you practice hypnosis. After practicing and learning a lot, you can consider yourself a hypnotist.

What Is Hypnosis?

Hypnosis is akin to the state of daydreaming, in which the conscious mind becomes quiet or passive. Through his practice, the hypnotist suggests the powerful subconscious mind of the subject.

Let's quickly and slightly technically examine how the brain works. Its activity is carried out in measurable frequency cycles that correspond to certain types of activity.

In 1929 Hans Berger used an EEG (electroencephalogram) system to discover that the brain produced normal waves in a sequence of 8 to 12 cycles per second (cps) while a person's eyes were closed. He called these waves alpha waves. Later, other types of brain waves were discovered, which were called theta, beta, and delta. These brain waves correspond to various mental functions, including hypnosis and psychic experience. Experts agree on the classification of these waves and their target but disagree regarding the exact limits of each wave type. An expert can define an alpha wave between 8 and 12 cps, while another can affirm that it is between 7 and 14 cps, and so on. The following four paragraphs provide a consensus regarding these brain waves.

Delta. For delta, the frequency spectrum of brain activation varies from 0 to around four cps. It is unconscious. There is not much knowledge about the delta range.

Theta. Theta frequency range is from about 4 to 7 cps. Theta is part of the subconscious range, and sometimes hypnosis takes place in this area. It seems that all our emotional experiences are registered in this wave. Theta is that special state that opens the door of consciousness beyond

231

hypnosis to the world of psychic phenomena. Psychic experience generally takes place in theta.

Alpha. The alpha frequency range is approximately 7 to 14 cps. Alpha is generally considered to be the subconscious zone. In one's dream, the daytime reverie, and practically all the hypnosis take place. Meditation and also the psychic experience occur mainly in alpha (although in the state of meditation occasionally theta is reached). Alpha is a very important region when it comes to hypnosis.

Beta. It is the conscious area of the mind with frequency ranges from 14 cps. Beta is where our reasoning takes place and conducts most of our occupations when we are awake. Almost all our activity is carried out mainly at about 20 cps. At approximately 60 cps, a person is in a state of acute hysteria. Above 60 cps, I don't know what could happen, but I suspect it wouldn't be pleasant at all.

When we go to sleep, our brain automatically descends from the beta to the alpha range and then, for brief periods, switches to theta and delta. Most of the dream takes place in alpha. Hypnosis abuses this natural phenomenon: it induces brain function to descend to the alpha level without the hypnotized person resting. The subconscious mind is open to the advice in alpha.

The conscious mind does not readily accept the suggestion. It is useful to reason and think, and also to put into action everything you know. The subconscious consciousness, though, is like an obedient slave. He does not think or understand; he reacts only to what is being said to him. In this lies the importance and strength of hypnosis, as it causes the message to be conveyed directly to the subconscious that embraces it and transforms it into fact. Also, the subconscious mind is reminding the conscious mind that there is and needs to be progress on new knowledge. The conscious mind is inclined to behave according to its contents, so it believes and behaves accordingly with the new knowledge. Though nobody understands why hypnosis is successful, and the subconscious mind is responding.

Suggestions

For now, you just need to know that it is extremely important that they are positive, constructive, and provide benefits. This is because the subconscious mind ignores the difference between a positive and a negative suggestion. The subconscious mind simply accepts what is offered to it and then acts accordingly.

Words used during the recommendation process ought to be very alert. A man used a filthy term composed of four letters hundreds of times a day, and it has a close meaning to defecating. He gradually told his subconscious he had to defecate, and constant diarrhea resulted. Words are very powerful, and the subconscious mind embraces them.

Myths

There are too many mistakes regarding hypnosis, many of which have been spread by movies that deal with people turned into zombies by an extremely powerful person who exclaims: "Look me in the eye!" This may be interesting, but it is mere fiction and has nothing to do with the truth. Below we will expose some of the most common myths and explain them:

A hypnotist has magical powers. This is false. A hypnotist is an ordinary human being who has prepared himself to use the power of suggestion to bring about certain desired results for the hypnotized person.

A hypnotist possesses supernatural abilities. That is completely wrong. A hypnotist is an average human being who has trained himself to use the power of persuasion to achieve the desirable effects for the hypnotized person.

A hypnotized person may do things against his or her will. Untrue. Second, they can't hypnotize someone against their will. That the subject wants to agree is necessary. Third, no hypnotized person will be compelled to do things they wouldn't do in a normal state. The subject may accept or refuse any suggested order during hypnosis. When what the hypnotist suggests disturbs the subject, the subject would be able to exit the hypnotic state in all likelihood.

Only weak-minded people will be hypnotized. Actually, the reverse is the case. The smarter a person is, the easier it is to hypnotize them. It is completely difficult to perform hypnosis in some instances of intellectual illness. Practically someone wanting to be hypnotized will be hypnotized. Due to mental disabilities or other causes outside our knowledge, about 1 percent of the population cannot be hypnotized.

.

An individual being hypnotized is in a trance or unconscious. False. A subject under hypnosis is awake and conscious: extremely conscious. What happens is that he has simply focused his attention on where the hypnotist has indicated and has abstracted himself from everything else.

Anyone can remain in a hypnotic state forever. This is completely false. Even assuming that the hypnotist died after hypnotizing the subject, the subject would easily leave the hypnotic state, either falling into a brief sleep and then waking up normally or opening their eyes by not listening for a while to the hypnotist's voice.

To obtain positive results, a state of deep hypnosis is required. It is not true. Any level of hypnosis can offer good results.

Hypnotic state

Anyone undergoing hypnosis is very aware of where they are and what is happening. The subject listens to everything that happens while immersed in a state similar to daytime sleep, deeply relaxed. Often the body is numb or unaware of having a body.

Autohypnosis

It is possible to self-hypnotize. Many people do it daily to give themselves constructive orders. It is much easier to self-hypnotize if you have already had the experience of being hypnotized by someone else and have been instructed to do so. Through this chapter, you will learn to hypnotize other people, but with the same instructions, you will learn to self-hypnotize yourself. If you work with someone who hypnotizes you, you will accelerate the learning process of self-hypnosis.

CHAPTER 18

HYPNOTHERAPY

So far, hypnotherapy has only achieved a few scientifically recognized successes, but it can still be used as an alternative healing method in many areas. Although conventional medicine is still skeptical, there are many people who firmly believe in the effectiveness of hypnosis. We will tell you how hypnotherapy works, whether it can actually work small miracles and how much such therapy costs.

Hypnotherapy: This is how the therapy works

Hypnosis takes advantage of the state of consciousness of the trance. In the trance, our selective thinking is switched off, which makes it possible to make suggestions to the patient.

Our subconscious is addressed during the trance. The subconscious stores all habits and is also our long-term memory. Reflexes, our breathing and the autonomic nervous system are controlled unconsciously. Our consciousness, on the other hand, is responsible for short-term memory, decisions and our will. The reason why good resolutions fail so often: our habits are stronger than our will!

There are various initiation techniques to achieve the trance state:

- In classic hypnotherapy, direct instructions are passed on to the patient; this can be achieved with the help of verbal suggestions, fictional stories, acoustic signals, imaginary images or physical sensations (warmth, heaviness).
- Indirect hypnotherapy based on the Ericksonian model uses subliminal instructions. This maintains the feeling of control for the patient and the change in consciousness occurs unexpectedly.
- Nonverbal trance induction is often combined with verbal. During mesmerizing, the state of trance is initiated by energy transfer, i.e. by sweeping along without touching the arms or legs. If the patient fixes a certain point in the room or on the face of the hypnotist, one speaks of fixation.

Flash hypnosis is not advisable; this state of trance only lasts briefly and is only used for entertainment in show hypnosis.

By repeating sequences of sentences and numbers or images, the hypnotist enables the trance to be deepened. The aim is to promote the greatest possible relaxation and to start troubleshooting in this state.

At the end of a session there is the withdrawal, in which you are brought back fully to consciousness by repeating stories, pictures or sequences of numbers in reverse order.

In these cases, hypnotherapy could help you

Although hypnotherapy can be used in many areas, you should be aware that it cannot replace conventional medical treatment for serious diseases such as cancer.

Especially in the psychotherapeutic area, hypnotherapy can improve the quality of life by overcoming anxiety and attachment disorders, depression and conflicts with oneself.

Hypnosis is also suitable as pain therapy accompanying chemotherapy, after surgery and for migraines and inflammatory bowel diseases. Success can also be achieved with addiction problems.

Hypnotherapy can also be successful in people who are afraid of exams or who are about to burn out, or at least serve as relaxation therapy.

How effective is hypnotherapy?

According to the German Medical Gazette, the effectiveness has been scientifically recognized by the German Medical Association.

Withdrawal from methadone (heroin substitute, which alleviates withdrawal pain) and smoking cessation can be demonstrated by hypnotherapy.

Furthermore, the effectiveness of hypnosis in diseases such as migraines and irritable bowel is proven by the Scientific Advisory Board on Psychology.

Why do few people get involved in hypnotherapy?

Many people are very afraid of losing control in a trance-like state. However, this fear is mostly unfounded, because we do not act against our habits and morals even in the subconscious.

For successful hypnotherapy, one should also believe in the effectiveness of the alternative healing method and not avoid the incomprehensible from the outset.

The costs of treatment are usually not covered by the statutory health insurance, private patients should discuss the assumption of costs in advance. A hypnosis session costs around 80 to 120 euros for 50 minutes. Depending on the clinical picture, you should expect three to seven sessions, but treatment over several years may also be necessary.

Most psychological, mental, and physical conditions may be treated with hypnotherapy. This is used for relieving chronic pain, persistent acute pain, pain from psychosomatic disorders (e.g., headaches, migraines, fibromyalgia, cancer pain, etc.), planning for delivery, and decreasing pain relievers.

In psychotherapy, it is effective for the treatment of mood disorders (including depression) and various anxiety disorders: panic attacks, specific phobia, and social phobia, post-traumatic stress disorder (PTSD), obsessive-compulsive disorder (OCD), etc.

Moreover, hypnotherapy is particularly indicated to reduce stress and overcome addictions such as smoking and alcoholism. Children are also easy to hypnotize, and bedwetting and chronic asthma can be improved by hypnotherapy.

With most psychological and emotional issues, hypnotherapy is one of the easiest, quickest, and most successful types of care. It encourages an independence and pride mentality to deal with challenges and can also improve the healing process for many physiological problems.

Where to find psychologists trained in hypnosis

Hypnosis is also a psychotherapeutic method and should thus not be used in isolation but instead incorporated into psychotherapy. When you are interested in benefiting from this therapy, you have to be aware that not everybody who has practiced this approach is qualified to be able to cope with psychological issues.

To provide the full assurance of therapeutic hypnosis, hypnotherapists must be trained in psychological therapy, in addition to specialists in hypnosis. The El Prado Psychologists Center in Madrid, which has some of the best psychologists specializing in hypnosis, is one of the clinics that are at the forefront of this method of care.

El Prado Psychologists Center is a clinic in psychology provided by the Community in Madrid as a health center. It has a team of hypnotherapists with comprehensive clinical hypnosis training and experience who use this technique to treat different problems. The Prado Psychologists will give you ideas and help you solve the challenges you are facing, so you can recover your emotional equilibrium and live a complete and rewarding life.

Many therapeutic approaches are successful.

While we frequently equate psychological counseling with a severe problem, for the most varied reasons, many people go to the psychologist: developing social skills, getting to know each other better, optimizing personal growth or enhancing communication with their spouse. This clinic does not preclude any psychotherapeutic model, as it aims to be better able to administer individual psychological care.

The intervention approach stands out for delivering concise interventions. As a learning hub, it is at the forefront of psychology, applying the latest developments in science and integrating brain improvement methods into psychotherapy, such as brain integration techniques (ICT) or mindfulness.

CHAPTER 19

BRAINWASHING

Brainwashing, also known as reform of thought, education, or re-education, is the application of techniques often coercive to change beliefs, behavior, thinking, and behavior of an individual or society, for political purposes, religious or any other. Some common brainwashing techniques are the constant repetition of the same message along with public derision or the demonization of anyone who contradicts the message. Others include tactics aimed at nullifying critical thinking as well as preventing access to uncensored sources of information, isolation from the outside world, manipulation of language and the use of labels.

General

Throughout history, various forms of control of the thinking of individuals have been used. But it has been the totalitarian societies of the 20th century that have first applied scientific knowledge to improve brainwashing techniques. And that today is supported frequently with the use of drugs that inhibit cognitive abilities, hunger and protein deprivation, which produces confusion and credulity in the reasoning ability; and sleep deprivation, which causes stress and confusion.

George Orwell, in his 1984 novel, described various techniques used in brainwashing. The effect of these techniques on the person's image is not perceived by most people subjected to brainwashing. One's image is mainly established from two sources:

- The outside world made up of their parents, their educators, their friends, and all the people who have crossed the path of their existence.
- Their thoughts.

Brainwashing seeks to create a social framework or an environment of ideas and models to follow, to which the individual must adapt to survive, be accepted, or feel integrated into the group or society in which they live.

What Is Brainwashing?

Brainwashing is a method, more or less effective depending on the individual, whose objective is to admit any information to another person, with the technique of repetition until the objective is reached. Sometimes verbal or physical violence is used to confirm or create a defined hierarchy of superiority between the scrubber and the person being brainwashed.

There is also talk of brainwashing carried out by the media on the population, which can effectively have the effect of imposing the media's point of view on the population in the long term. The best way to avoid control of information is to use several sources within the possible informative spectrum.

Although the word "sect" is related to groups that have the same affinity, over the years, it has acquired a connotation more related to radicalized groups. Generally religious, tending to control thinking other than their own, outside and within their organization. It is present like this within some sects: brainwashing, mind control, persecution, human and sexual exploitation, slavery, and various forms of abuse. From a sociological point of view, it is a group of people with common affinities (cultural, religious, political, esoteric, etc.). Usually, it is a pejorative term, against which it has emerged, that of "new religious movements."

Brainwashing in the 21st Century

Brainwashing in the masses

The term brainwashing is sometimes applied, in

some societies, when the government maintains firm social control of the mass media and the education system and uses this control to disseminate propaganda on a particularly intensive scale, with the global effect that can brainwash large sections of the population. This political interest manipulation can be seen in the case of, for example, the Soviet Union, China, or Israel, where all information is subjected to intense censorship and education.

The so-called Propaganda seeks to influence the citizen's value system and their behavior. It is articulated from a persuasive discourse that seeks public adherence to its interests. It is monological in nature and requires the resource of the advertisement. Its approach is to use massively presented and disseminated information to support a certain ideological or political opinion. Although the message contains true information, it may be incomplete, not contrasted, and partisan (disinformation), so that it does not present a balanced picture of the opinion in question, which is always viewed in an asymmetric, subjective and emotional way. Its primary use comes from the political context, generally referring to government or party sponsored efforts to convince the masses.

Thought Reform

The change of thinking or coercion, as it is often called, is an attenuated synonym for brainwashing. It is better understood as an organized method of phased coercive manipulation and regulation of behavior, intended to persuade and affect people deceptively and unexpectedly. This is usually in a scene orchestrated by the organization, for the benefit of the program's designers.

Brainwashing in youth

Brainwashing is much more effective when applied to young individuals than to those who already have a formed personality. Several programs are established in the subject during childhood, at an age when his critical sense is still very little developed, and he easily and naturally accepts all the suggestions coming from outside. These suggestions, the basis of the program, come at the beginning from the parents, later adding other adults, educators, and the individuals with whom the child is related, who may be of the same age, or even younger and of another sex.

For example, the US government uses the Holocaust Museum, built-in Washington DC with public funds, to teach hundreds of thousands of schoolchildren who visit it, at an age when the critical sense is not yet developed. Therefore, those beliefs will become deeply embedded. The German government, for its part, maintains a list of books on politics, prohibited for young people (see the case of the censorship of the writer Udo Walendy). In this way, he prevents his unscrupulous plan of political indoctrination of children and young people in classrooms on issues such as the Holocaust.

Deprogramming

Deprogramming is the process of releasing someone from the mind control to which he has been subjected. Since control is a long and complex technique, so is deprogramming; for this reason, some professionals are well versed in the field.

Circumstances

To achieve deprogramming, especially the most destructive control, the concurrence of several circumstances is necessary:

- Separation of the controlling group.
- Physical rest.
- Adequate food.
- Perseverance.

Techniques

Once the above circumstances have been met, experts in the field such as Steven Hassan follow a series of deprogramming techniques:

1. Establish relationships of mutual trust.
2. Communicate with the person to know their situation (do you want to continue? Do you feel doubts about the goodness of those who have controlled you? Are you disenchanted but fearful?...).
3. Developing identity models: what the person was like before entering, how does mind control impose the personality model, and what is the personality that it adopts within the controlling structure (initiated, with some responsibility, controller...).
4. Putting people in touch with the original identity; that's why it's so difficult to deprogram children, who have no previous personality to recover.
5. Change the perspective from which the controller looks (the one imposed by the controller group).
6. Disrupt the self-deception that the controlled person has been systematically taught to do when they have doubts about what they have been taught.

7. End the phobias that have been implanted in the person so that he does not leave the group and show him the well-being that can be obtained outside the group.
8. Explain to the controlled person the characteristics of the mental control he has suffered.

CHAPTER 20

SOCIAL INFLUENCE

Social influence occurs when a person's emotions, opinions, or behaviors are affected by others. Social influence takes many forms and can be seen in compliance, socialization, peer pressure, obedience, leadership, persuasion, sales, and marketing. In 1958, Harvard psychologist Herbert Kelman identified three-wide varieties of social influence.

Social influence

In the face of a persuasive message, the recipient can:

- Process the message rationally.
- Let yourself be carried away by heuristics.

For some authors such as Allport, social influence is the central object of study in Social Psychology. Allport defines the study of social influence: I try to understand and explain how the thoughts, feelings, and behaviors of individuals are influenced by the real, imagined, or implicit presence of others. People intervene, sometimes as an influential agent, sometimes as a target that is influenced by other human beings. Influence is not always deliberate or explicit.

Intended Social Influence or Persuasion

Through the processes of influence and persuasion, our affections, beliefs, attitudes, intentions, and behaviors are configured. The intention to influence is always aimed at achieving a change in the behavior of others, individuals, or groups. Sometimes the objective is to achieve a specific behavior (that they prepare breakfast for us); other times, it is intended to influence attitudes (announcement of nature). Attempts to influence can occur: In face-to-face processes or through the media.

Typologies in The Study of Influence

DEPENDING ON THE OBJECTIVE OF THE INFLUENCING AGENT: a) Achieve specific behavior in the receiver. b) Get them to change their attitudes to produce, in the long run, a behavioral change.

DEPENDING ON THE SCENARIO in which it takes place:

Direct or face-to-face interpersonal communication: The interaction is bidirectional and dialectical. The influencer and his target intervene at the same time. The influence target participates by imposing his position.

Direct communication directed to an audience: One-way and little reciprocal interaction (meeting). The influence target can be expressed through reactions (applause, booing), but its influence on the agent of influence is less.

Mass communication: There is no direct contact between the communicator and the audience. The influence is unidirectional.

Social psychology analyzes the psychological processes involved in interpersonal influence and the most effective influence tactics. It helps to understand better why people behave in a certain way, to defend against manipulation, and to get experts in influencing techniques.

Influence techniques

People use tactics when we want to influence.

ROBERT CIALDINI systematized all the influencing techniques observed about a series of psychological principles. Psychological principles are understood as fundamental characteristics of the human being from which many social behaviors are derived, or that serve as a guide to act in different interaction situations. Since they are useful in interaction processes, it is easy for them to work when trying to trigger a certain response.

These tactics can be grouped, according to the underlying psychological principle, into 6 PRINCIPLES OF INFLUENCE:

Principle of reciprocity: "We have to treat others as they treat us." It is easier to convince those people who have previously been given a gift or a favor to support our purposes.

Scarcity principle: "What is most difficult to achieve is valued." Any opportunity seems more attractive to us, the less affordable it presents itself (due to its economic cost or the effort involved). Principle of social validation: Tendency to act like the people around us do. In most cases, it is usually appropriate to do what people similar to us do.

Principle of sympathy: Tendency to do what the people we like, or love want to do. The greater the attraction that a person arouses, the greater the possibility that he has to influence. The principle of authority: Obligation to obey the boss. Obedience, not only to legitimate authority but also to symbols associated with authority. Coherence principle: Importance of being consistent with previous actions and with previously acquired commitments.

Common characteristics of the previous principles:

- They are useful in most cases.
- They are rules of coexistence highly valued socially.
- They are learned from childhood.
- They serve as a heuristic or cognitive shortcut to quickly interpret and act in a social situation.
- They are usually used by conviction professionals to achieve their purposes.

The fact that they are used as heuristics means that they provoke automatic responses. This type of answer has the advantage that it saves time and mental capacity, and the disadvantage that it increases the possibility of error. Depending on the characteristics of the interaction, some principles work better than others.

The effectiveness of influence tactics depends on the influence agent using them appropriately for the situation and the people involved in the interaction. The joint use of more than one principle maximizes the possibilities of influencing.

CHAPTER 21

THE SECRETS OF SUBLIMINAL PSYCHOLOGY

The theme of subliminal messages in music began to gain importance in the early 1970s when various religious movements claimed that they were capable of unconsciously influencing people and changing their behavior. Even today, there is controversy about it.

The subject of subliminal messages in music has always been surrounded by controversy. For some, it is a simple myth, for others, a minor anecdote. Some think that it is a manipulation mechanism that is capable of changing people's behavior and influencing their values.

There is still no definitive conclusion in this regard, neither about the subliminal messages in music nor in those that have to do with the image. The available data is contradictory. Several governments have banned this type of message, but at the same time, most researchers have distorted its real effectiveness.

The subject has become fashionable at times and has caused everything from laughter to enormous concerns. At times, it has been pointed out that subliminal messages in music incite crime, practice Satanism, use drugs, etc. How true is this?

Some history

Let's say first that subliminal messages are those that are designed to be captured below the normal limits of perception. In other words, these messages cannot be consciously perceived but are received in such a way that we do not realize that we are capturing them.

Everything indicates that these messages have been spoken for thousands of years. Specifically, there are allusions by Aristotle to impulses that go unnoticed when we are awake, but then reappear strongly when we are asleep. Michell de Montaigne, O. Poetzle, and later Sigmund Freud also referred to this type of unconscious phenomenon.

However, advances in technology made these phenomena much more evident. Thus, it was in the 20th century when it became really clear that this type of communication was possible.

In 1957, a famous experiment was done with images, and almost a decade later, The Beatles got everyone to talk about subliminal messages in music or backmasking.

Subliminal messages in music

Subliminal messages in music, or backmasking, are encoded using a recording technique. It consists of recording a sound or message backward, on a track that is designed to be heard forward. This means that such a message can only be consciously picked up if the track is run backward.

There were two decisive factors in the birth of subliminal messages in music. The first was the rise of "concrete music" in France. In this genre, the sounds of electronic instruments were combined with recorded sounds from the environment or industry and combined in the recording studio.

The second incident factor was the use of recording tapes to record and preserve the musicians' original performances. This allowed fragments to be combined, cut, overlaid, and pasted to the original recording.

The Beatles and John Lennon, in particular, did several experiments around concrete music, and a new story began there.

The seventh Beatles album included, for the first time, a song that had texts recorded backward. The theme was called Rain, and it appeared in 1966. The objective of the band was to satirize, experiment, and offer new sounds. Since then, a good number of artists have resorted to the same resource, and subliminal messages in music have become frequent.

Doubts that persist

Quickly, several religious movements began to speak out against this type of appeal. Several urban legends also began to gain strength. Many people listened to the tapes backward and found hidden meanings, but most of the time, they were pure guesses, without a concrete basis.

The religious, in particular, accused various rock groups of inducing youth to worship the devil, commit crimes, or use drugs. The debate became very heated until, in 1985, the psychologists' John R. Vokey and J. Don Read experimented. They recorded a Psalm from the Bible upside down and watched the listeners' reactions.

The researchers concluded that subliminal messages in music did not cause any considerable effect on the receivers. In 1996 C. Trappery did 23 experiments and concluded the same thing. However, researchers Johan C. Karremansa, Wolfgang Stroebeb, and Jasper Claus, from the University of Utrecht, did a new experiment in 2006 and proved that these messages do change people's behavior. The debate is still open.

Subliminal Psychology in An Intimate Relationship

We know individuals appear to be drawn to, to make appointments, and to marry other people who are similar to them in terms of personality and values, in addition to their physical appearance. However, these characteristics only scratch the surface of what makes a relationship work well. The agreement in certain aspects of the style of speaking of each member of the couple is also important, according to the results of a new study in which it has been found that people who speak in a similar way regarding certain parameters are more compatible with forming a lasting couple.

The study focused on what is technically known as "function words." It is not about nouns and verbs; but the words that show how those others are related. How we use these words constitutes our style of speaking and writing, according to James Pennebaker of the University of Texas at Austin.

Function words are very social, and social skills are required to use them. For example, "the other day's" may be very clear to two people when one says it to the other, but a third person who hears them may not have the slightest idea what they mean.

Pennebaker, Molly Ireland, and colleagues examined whether the speaking and writing styles couples adopt during one member's conversations with the other predict future dating behavior and the long-term strength of their relationship. The study authors conducted two experiments in which software compared the language styles of the couples.

In the first experiment, the conversations of pairs of college students whose members had four-minute speed dating were recorded to meet and see if they liked each other. Almost all the couples talked about the same topics: What is your main subject? Where are you from? What do you think of the university? Each conversation sounded more or less the same to observers, but analysis of the spoken text revealed marked differences in the synchrony of language. Couples whose language style similarity was above average were nearly four times more likely than couples whose speech styles were out of line to expect to have further potential interactions.

A second analysis showed ten days of the same trend in online chat between couples. Nearly 80 percent of the couples whose two members' writing styles matched continued to date three months later, compared to approximately 54 percent of couples who did not match that style as much.

CHAPTER 22

HOW TO USE DARK PSYCHOLOGY IN SEDUCTION

The art of seduction is something that many long to understand and practice efficiently, and that seduction is not always for sexual gain. Unlike what many may think, it is something deeper and more complex than it seems at first glance.

A true seducer or seductress is that person capable of arousing interest in others for elements of their personality, their attractiveness, their way of expressing themselves, knowledge, etc. Many of the seducers are attractive without having a sexual interest different from the rest. However, they are capable of producing a feeling of trust in people, motivating others to do what they want, or achieving a benefit that nurtures both parties.

Seducer Features

Some studies indicate that from childhood, we acquire this capacity for seduction, but some train it better throughout their lives. We all know the typical person who, no matter where or how he is, manages to be the center of attention in a positive way without trying. These seducers produce interest or provocation in the rest in a very natural way.

The true seducer is one who seduces you without you realizing it. It can be their phrases, gestures, behaviors, education, security, etc. Each seducer has his tactics, all of them positive since they do not need to use tricks or bad arts to get what they want.

Contrary to what one might think, a seducer does not need to be particularly handsome, intelligent, funny, or overly daring. Sometimes, they don't even know what the "hook" they have with people is or why people are interested in them.

The problems seducers face

It could seem that seducers have it all in their favor and that they will run into little trouble. But the truth is otherwise. They can experience serious problems in all areas of their lives, especially in the emotional part.

When living with a seducer, problems such as jealousy, mistrust, or insecurity, among others, may arise. The couple's self-esteem will be vital to define the seriousness of these problems. A person sure of herself and the relationship will be able to bear the natural seduction of her partner and even take it with grace.

Otherwise, the seducer may face jealous scenes and unpleasant situations. The person who lives with the seducer must have high self-esteem, confidence in their partner, and the certainty that it is not the seducer who is looking for something, but other people who approach and express interest.

Enjoy the seducer

When you live with a seducer, you have to think positively because just what made you fall in love with him or her, will attract the attention of others. Learn to appreciate and be happy to be able to enjoy that person and his/her qualities.

CHAPTER 23

CONCLUSION

The dark triad is a term that emerged in the 1990s. Now, it was the studies and description of psychologists Paulhus and Williams of the University of British Columbia who coined this dimension in 2002. This should be noted as an important aspect.

When we speak of the dark triad, we are not referring to a personality disorder; they are a set of subclinical features that define a type of adverse behaviors, and that generate great discomfort in the environment.

A person who scores high in the dark triad test will generate a psychosocial impact in any scenario in which he moves. Thus, both family, emotional, and work-related relationships are affected by these antisocial tactics that these men and women make use of. Let us now analyze the signals of the dark triad.

We know that the signs of the dark triad of Psychology form a wide range. Does this mean that a person should score high in both narcissism, Machiavellianism, and psychopathy? Indeed, the score should be positive in all areas, but there are nuances. The Jonason and Webster scale is usually used to make an adequate evaluation.

In it, it can be seen that, on average, there is always one more significant area than others. An example: in a study carried out by Webster and Jonason (2013) at various universities in the United States, it was found that those with the highest scores in the narcissistic area abound.

Now, what this scale also reveals is that the most dangerous profile within the dark triad of personality is the one that shows a higher score in the area of psychopathy. In this case, it is when the most harmful and adverse behaviors appear. As we see, this is a subject as interesting as it is disturbing, especially when we consider what the psychoanalyst Michael Maccoby tells us: the dark triad of Psychology is increasingly common in the highest positions in the business field.